BackStage with Bryan Rooney

From Liverpool to Ringo to Donna Summer...

By Bryan Rooney

Copyright © 2008 by Ariey Production

All rights reserved. No part of this book may be reproduced, scanned, or distributed in any printed or electronic form without written permission of Ariey Production.

http://www.backstagestory.com

>   Rooney, Bryan P.
>
>   BackStage with Bryan Rooney: from Liverpool to Ringo to Donna Summer… / by Bryan Rooney – c2008.
>
>   Santa Clarita, CA.
>
>   ISBN 978-1-51175-115-5

Second printing

Editor and Book Designer: Colleen Spears.
Cover/Author Photo: Lily Qian-Falzone.
Center Photo Section: All photos courtesy Bryan Rooney.

To Jill and Gemma: You're what it's all about.

To Kenny Smith: Thanks for saving me—many times.

To Diane and Sue, my sisters: Thanks for finding me again.

To road crews everywhere, with dirty fingernails from actually working for a living, who would walk through a minefield to do a show...and make the spots on stage look and sound great: Bollocks!

God bless 'em, every single one of 'em.

Table of Contents

Foreword by Kenny Smith i
Note From Vince Falzone iii
Editor's Note vii

Introduction 1

In Liverpool and at Sea 3
    The Merchant Navy 7
    Back in Liverpool 11
    Prison for a Scooter Violation 13
    First Roadie Gig: St. James Infirmary 14

In London and on Tour with Procol Harum 17
    One of Two Roadies for Procol Harum 23
    Train Tour with Jimi Hendrix and the Grateful Dead 25
    The Isle of Wight Festival 29
    Frisian Islands Riot 31
    Rockin' and Rollin' to Berlin 32
    Fired from Procol Harum by Chrysalis 33

Germany: Touring with Reinhard Mey 39
    The Americans Next Door 40
    Learning German with Bob Nixon 41
    On Tour with Reinhard Mey 42
    Christmastime Alone in Düsseldorf 43

Working for The Beatles at Apple 47
    Back in London: Hired by Apple Corp. 50
    Tumbling Down George Harrison's Stairs 54
    Tending Bar for Ringo Starr 58
    Driving John Lennon's Psychedelic Rolls 59
    Meeting Paul McCartney 62

Helping Ringo's Assistant Kenny Smith 65
    Elvis for President 66
    Harry Nilsson: The *Real* Fifth Beatle 67
    Almost Fired by Allen Klein 68

Working at Tittenhurst Park 70
Ringo Buys All of Ludwig's Pigskins 72
How to Build a Lake in 3 Easy Steps 72
Fistfight with Rod Stewart 76
Son of Dracula Movie 77
An Irish Gypsy Vacation 78
Working for Ringo's Manager Hilary Gerrard 81

Photos 83

Los Angeles 105
Someone Else Tumbling Down Stairs 106
A Redhead Catches My Eye 107
Working for Ringo/Apple Again 109
Filling in for Keith Moon's Assistant 110
Tying the Knot at Ringo's Home 117
Sausage Delivery by Concorde 119

On Tour with Donna Summer 125
Stage Manager for Donna Summer 126
How I Lost My Front Teeth 128
Billionaire's Party—and Jail 131
Donna Summer's Adventure on Her Crew's Plane 136
Meeting El Presidente in Santo Domingo 144
Donna Treats Us to a Hawaiian Vacation 150
Reunited with My Sisters 152
Managing Donna's Sound Stage in L.A 153
Born Again? Nah! 154

Roadie Dad and Video Mum 159

Sickness and Recovery 165
Relapses 168

I Survived 171

Coda 175

Foreword

Liverpool was a fantastic place to be in the "Swingin' Sixties," what with the Cavern Club and all; but when The Beatles wrote, "Roll up for The Mystery Tour," my new friend Bryan and I decided that if we were to be at the front of the queue, we should move to London.

We shared a flat with five other lads from Liverpool, and with our music business skills, became freelance road managers. With our accents, our bravado and with the aid of the all-important screwdriver, torch, roll of gaffer tape and a passing "We're with the band," we could get into anywhere! We became members of The Speakeasy Club by claiming to be road managers of The Who! Life was good! I was fortunate to get a job at Apple working for Ringo Starr and soon after was able to get Bryan on the payroll. Can you imagine how popular you could be with an advance copy of *Abbey Road*? Life was getting better all the time.

Although Bryan and I went our separate ways in the mid '70s when he left for America, we continued our friendship and enjoyed many holidays and great times together.

I will never forget Bryan and the great adventures that we shared.

As the Fab Four said, it was indeed a "Long and Winding Road"—but, above all, a truly "Magical Mystery Tour."

Kenny Smith
December 29, 2006
Music industry veteran Kenny Smith is well known for early work as Ringo Starr's assistant, and later managing The Eurythmics.

Note From Vince Falzone

The day I met Bryan Rooney in 2005 was supposed to be just another Friday evening radio interview for me with our local hometown radio station, KHTS AM-1220, in Santa Clarita, CA. Usually during the weekly interview I talk about my music and the things that are going on with me in a 10-minute segment called "A Day in the Life with Vince Falzone, Local Singer, Songwriter, and Guitarist."

But this would turn out to be a prolific evening for me. Being a huge Beatles fan, I was about to "meet" each one of The Beatles during the time and place they ruled music: the late 1960s to early 1970s in London, England. But that's not possible; or is it? Could there be yet another side of music history we have not heard?

Bryan Rooney most certainly has some insight on that and much more. He worked for Apple Records and became good friends with one of his employers, Ringo Starr, who was eventually the best man at Bryan's wedding to Jill, which is also where he met future employer Donna Summer just before she became one of the hottest artists of the 1980s.

So here I am walking up to the radio's booth in our local mall as the group before me, SCV-Arts is finishing up their 10-minute segment. I listen to KHTS interviewing this guy with a Liverpool accent and wonder who he is. I see various photos laid out, and a folder of other photos, some of which appear to be very old black-and-white shots, while others seem like they are from the 1970s and are printed out in color on large photo paper. I hear the name Ringo Starr mentioned quite a bit and start to wonder if this guy *is* Ringo, with the distinctive Liverpool accent all Beatles fans have come to know (and mimic, as my friends and I did while growing up in South Florida). I notice the guy's United Kingdom Union Jack flag shirt. Then the florescent green dress shoes beneath his jeans grab my eyes and I begin to feel like I am in some sort of time warp. Still not sure who this person is, I keep looking at the wedding photos with Ringo and a few others dressed in 1970s bell-bottom pants and shirts with large collars.

After his interview is over, I say "Hello," and he says, "Hello! What's your name, mate?" As I reply, "My name is Vince Fal—," he says, "Oho! I've heard of you. You're that musician guy." I smile and say, "Who are you?" He says, "I am Bryan Rooney, and I used to work for The Beatles and Apple Records during the early 1970s, and loads of other lads like Procol Harum, Keith Moon, and Jimi Hendrix. And if you have some time I can tell you some stories about them." Like that's not enough to entice any music fan, I say, "Sure." He's finished his interview and I have a few minutes before my own interview starts.

We sit down and Bryan starts telling me about how he lost his front teeth during a riot in Italy while running sound for a Donna Summer concert. Then he tells me about how nice a person Ringo Starr was while Bryan worked and lived at Tittenhurst Park when Ringo owned the place. The stories continue and seem to be too good to be true, so I begin to quiz him about The Beatles…and hear him tell me stuff about them as if it happened a few minutes ago. I realize this guy is an amazing storyteller, and if these stories of his are true, they need to be heard by anyone who loves music. I mean, VH1 is airing *The Osbournes* with Ozzy, Sharon, Kelly and Jack—and Bryan's stuff is, in my opinion, much more insightful if you're a musician or into music. This information is about the people and artists behind the scenes (or as I call it, "BackStage").

Bryan Rooney was a roadie who went from box pusher for a small Liverpool band to production manager for Donna Summer during her world tour in the disco era. He knew and worked for The Beatles, met

The Rolling Stones…and that was just the first few minutes I talked with him.

Then I tell Bryan he needs to write a book about this stuff, because 30 minutes flew by and I simply wanted to hear more from him, but my own interview was about to start. He says, "Well, I thought about writing a book…but…, I can't write. I think that's the problem." Off the cuff I reply, "Well, I'll write it for you." He says, "I like you. That will be just fine! When do we start?" Kind of in shock from what I just heard, I try to process this information, this, "Sure, go ahead and write 'my life working for famous artists and such.'" I put my hands up like a TV producer and realize I need to interview and film him before he tells me any more.

The photo with this section was taken with a camera phone the day I met Bryan. It will forever be a day I will not forget.

Vince Falzone

June 2007

Vince Falzone is a professional musician. He has released 8 CDs to date, and has weekly radio and TV shows in the Los Angeles area.

For more information on Vince, visit
http://www.MusicByVince.com.

For more information on the BackStage project,
to watch video clips of Bryan Rooney telling his stories in person,
or to order a DVD of Bryan's interviews with Vince
for this book, visit
http://www.BackStageStory.com.

Editor's Note

The words you read on the following pages are all Bryan's. They give you an introductory taste of his masterful, charming storytelling—although only this project's video and audiotaped interviews could truly capture his tone, expressions, and what we Americans consider his heavy English accent. How to write down the ever-present devilish glint in his eyes, the cigarettes he gestured with? How to show on the page that he pronounced former employer Ringo Starr's name as "Rrringo," and former boss Donna Summer's name as "Donnar"? As you'll see on the clips at BackStageStory.com, Bryan could be effortlessly entertaining for hours on end.

Despite his incredible memory for visual details and ability to make you feel you are there with him in his escapades, Bryan was not someone who remembered dates. For most of his life he focused entirely on the present, and proudly said that for decades he didn't even own a watch, and sometimes didn't know (or care) what day, month, or year it was.

Although extensive efforts were made to verify this manuscript's details, names, and dates, Bryan suddenly passed away with only half of the initial round of revisions completed.

This book presents Bryan's stories as he told them to us. Therefore, concerning the content herein, although we at BackStage have made reasonable efforts to include accurate information, we make no warranties or representations whatsoever, and assume no liability, obligation, or responsibility for the opinions expressed, nor the content's accuracy or completeness.

In a classic understatement, Bryan's wife Jill once said, "He lived a very full life." How many of us can truly say the same about our own lives?

We sincerely hope you will enjoy Bryan Rooney's life story as much as we did.

Colleen Spears
June 2007

Introduction

One particular day while I was living in Monte Carlo with Ringo Starr and his girlfriend Nancy, Ringo said, "Oh, God, I've got all these papers, they've gotta be in New York."

I said, "Oh, okay, fine."

"It's an emergency: They've *gotta* get to New York. I've just signed them. They've gotta be in New York. It's part of this big contract."

"Okay."

"So," he says, "get to London, and then get to New York as soon as you can, because the office has other paperwork for ya too."

"Okay, no problem." That was my job.

I jump a plane to London, and get one of the guys to come pick me up and take me to Apple to pick up more paperwork before I find a plane to New York. While I'm at the office waiting for the final envelope for New York, someone says, "Bryan, there's a call for ya."

The phone rings in my little cubbyhole. "Hello?"

"'Allo, Bryan! How's it going?" It was John Lennon, calling from New York.

"Oh, yeah! All right, man! What's the story?"

He says, "Aw, great! I need ya…to get some sausages for me. And get 'em to me as soon as possible." English sausages are a special thing. You just can't get 'em in America. He didn't know I'd just flown in from Monte Carlo with paperwork from Ringo that had to go to New York. I think he just phoned the office 'cause he thought I'd be around.

John says, "I *need* some sausages. Gotta have 'em. I have my account at…."

1

"Oh, yeah, I know your butcher." Everybody had accounts, had their own private butchers, hairdressers, apple-growers, etc. There were so many accounts, no wonder Apple had so many accountants! It didn't matter what you wanted, you didn't have to pay for it, you just signed for it.

He said, "I've *gotta* have 'em!"

"Well, as it happens, I'm goin' to New York."

"Right! Great! Get up to the butcher shop, get 10 pounds of sausages, stick 'em in your briefcase, and I'll take care of the customs at this end." Never mind the paperwork I've got. And that you're not supposed to be bringin' fresh meat into America.

"Okay…. Yeah."

He said, "Well…, get it! Do it, now!"

"Well, the fastest way is the Concorde."

"Good thinkin'! Do it! Get the Concorde." The Concorde were new at that time, and cost thousands upon thousands of dollars to fly on. John goes, "Just get on the bloody Concorde and get 'ere, now."

It fit in with the paperwork I had to deliver for Ringo, so I said, "Okay!"

In Liverpool and at Sea

I'm from Liverpool, the Detroit of England. It's a cold, hard, gray port with lots of lovely people. I was born June 3, 1949, just 4 years after World War II.

My father Richard was in the ground staff of the Royal Air Force (RAF); my mother Kathleen was working with the Women's Auxiliary Air Force (WAAF), a charity, helping neighbors. That's how they met, I believe. Got married in 1944, had children.

After the war my parents were no longer in the military, but lived at an old military camp near Liverpool, Leyfield Estate. It had been closed down as an airfield, but people were allowed live there because there was no housing—so much had been bombed.

When I was born we were living in an old barracks on the military camp in a Nissen shed, a corrugated tin hut with a couple of windows. Cheap and cheerful. The dirt floor had a great big 6-foot-diameter hole in the ground for a bomb shelter. There were communal baths and bathrooms. I'm fortunate that I have 2 sisters who remember everything, so they've filled me in quite a lot on my toddler days. Like the funniest thing was me falling down the hole in the barracks room. It probably wasn't funny to my mum, or my father, but that's what I did for the first couple years of my life: Fall in holes. Aside from the hole in our hut, there were craters all over the bloody airfield from former gun emplacements and bombs, some with unexploded shells in them. It was a bit dodgy to play there. Liverpool wasn't as badly bombed as London, but they did try to bomb Liverpool because it's a port.

In 1950 we moved out to the suburbs of Liverpool, to Norris Green, 22 Busby Road, then the next year to West Derby, 1 Aspes Road. There were millions of people in the war effort, but afterwards they all went back to their lives. My mother was a homemaker. My father was a craftsman who created beautiful handmade cabinets. We had a small house, but it was nice.

My youth was just…Liverpool. There was the rag-and-bone man who'd come 'round with a horse and cart to buy our rags every Tuesday. You'd hear the bell and took your old clothes, lamb bones and dog bones out to him and he'd weigh 'em, and he'd give you a couple of coins, a balloon, or a goldfish. Like a mobile Goodwill. I'd bring my sisters' clothes just to get a balloon…and then I'd get in real trouble.

English schools had grades 2 through 10. I was in a free government nursery school from the age of 2, because we were still recovering from the war, and everybody was working, including mothers. So I went to nursery school, played with crayons, chased the girls with pigtails, had my afternoon naps at one o'clock. My mom would come and pick me up and we'd walk 4 miles home with holes in our shoes. Really. We'd walk everyplace. Everybody did in those days.

My sister Diane is 2 years older, and Susan is 3 years younger. You'd think my parents were poets, especially my Irish dad, who was very lyrical: Di-ane, Bry-an, Sus-an. It stood out in a crowd of relatives. So I was the little Irish male in the middle. Yes, I'm an Irishman more than an Englishman, because my father was Irish. And males get away with murder in an Irish society. The men were the priests, or the ones who brought home the money, and they got the biggest servings of food. Even as I child I was shown favoritism, which my sisters did not like at all. They didn't consider being male any kind of cultural advantage. If there was any trouble going around, it was the sisters who would be in trouble. I would escape punishment because I was the male.

A ways back, when the Spanish Armada came to invade England in 1588, my great-great-great-etc. grandfather on my mother's side married a Spanish lady off one of the Spanish ships that got wrecked. She was a Countessa, which gives me the merest drop of royal Spanish blood.

My father smoked, and died of lung cancer in 1954, when I was 4. So I never really knew him that well, as a child or as a son. I have photographs of him…and a handsome devil he is!

As a widow and a war veteran, my mother had a pension from the government, which was not a lot to keep 3 growing kids going. She worked at the Catholic church. We were supposed to be in bed by 8, before she got home. We knew which bus she'd be on, the #12, so we'd play out in the street until we saw it in the distance. Then we'd dive through the hedge and run upstairs, jump in bed fully clothed and pull the covers up to our chins and fake sleep. Mum was strict, but not unfair. We'd act up and get a good slap on the knuckles with a ruler, or a leather belt for that matter. But nothing that would damage you. It would just get you ready for convent school, when the nuns would take over.

The discipline in a Catholic school that's run by nuns is akin to going to Borstal, which is a detention center. It's very heavy. You weren't allowed just to mess up. You sat, and you moved when you were supposed to. You did your lessons, and if you messed up, *bam*! You'd have nice red knuckles to go home. And then your mother would say, "What happened to your knuckles? You've been in trouble again." And you might get a clip around the head as a bonus. But then it's done, no more hitting. It'd be over and done with. Until the next time.

My first public Catholic school after I got away from the convent was St. Dominick's, which had a huge church connected to it, almost as big as a cathedral. Religion was part of the educational system, unlike the U.S. where it all has to be separate. In those days, in Ireland, the Catholic and Protestant camps were blowin' each other up, and Liverpool was like a capsule of Ireland. When I was a kid, you knew everybody—what school, what church, what pub, where they bought groceries, where they ate, what they smoked. And we were not allowed to talk to Protestant kids, and vice versa.

As an altar boy I used to do Sunday mass every week. I spoke minimal Latin, enough to do a mass: "*Pater noster qui es in caelis, sanctificetur nomen tuum, adveniat regnum tuum.*" That's the start of the "Our Father." Latin is a dead language, but they taught it to Catholic altar boys because the priests served mass in that language, so you had to know what was going on so you could do your various things throughout the mass: communion, giving the priest his wine, etc. It was an hour-and-a-half or 2-hour event every Sunday. Everything had to be perfect. Your white surplice had to be starched, your shoes polished. And of course my mother was ever-so-proud that I was an altar boy. It was like I was going in the right direction.

The churches in England were part of the social situation, because nobody had anything. The churches were there to help. You got a meal for polishing the piano. Or polish the pews and they'd give you a bag of crisps. I think my sisters did some shop work, retail. We went on, one day to the next.

The main difference I noticed in friends' families with fathers was that they had more stuff. Maybe they could afford a 12" television. Nobody had cars. We walked everywhere. I walked 4 miles to school every day. And back. The school had a free government lunch program. My mum would give us money for the bus, which we never rode. We walked it, and kept the money for candy.

Even a few years after the war, you couldn't buy a bar of chocolate. England was still rationing—cigarettes, candy, bread. You needed your little ration book, and gave it to the confectioner. Whatever your little ticket said, that's what you were allowed, plus a few pennies for the shopkeeper. We got by.

The schools had after-class activities like woodwork and metalwork shops. I built a big wooden touring kayak with a canvas deck. I had friends help me. The school supplied the wood, the Boy Scouts supplied the plans.

I joined the Chess Club and I was quite rated in Liverpool at one point. Our Chess Club was quite good, which is where I learned how you win: by being sneaky. Nasty. My wife will confirm that. Obviously I play by the rules, but there are ways of doing it that the other guy doesn't know about, or really think beyond what you're doing. You could be 10 moves ahead in your thinking. That's what they taught me, and I enjoyed it. My wife still won't play chess with me because she thinks I'm devious....

Sometimes the whole school went camping, which was like taking a circus on the road. We'd go down to southern England, to Teinmouth in Devon. It's relatively warm, after Liverpool: They grow palm trees there.

I finished school when I was 15 or so. You could carry on—if you had the right aptitude—to trade school, college, university, whatever. The school system had particular exams called A-Levels, and you had to have X amount of points within the A-Levels before you could apply to a college or a trade school. I didn't. I just went to work.

My mother had friends in the Merchant Navy Catering School. So I actually did go to a 10-month trade school, but only for 6 weeks, because the union guy running the school was my mother's boyfriend. He gave me the answers to all the tests and put down that I finished.

So 6 weeks after joining a trade school, one fine and frosty morning in 1964, I was on a bus, on my own, with a little suitcase. My Mum stood there and waved as the bus pulled away. I went to the docks to find my huge Merchant Navy ship, the Sylvania.

The Merchant Navy

As a port on England's western coast, Liverpool was like a gateway city from Ireland. That's how my father got there. And most people fleeing Ireland for America had to come to Liverpool first. We'd sail from Liverpool to southern Ireland to pick up some more Irish refugees, then head for America.

Sometimes we'd go to America via Newfoundland, or St. John, in Canada, which are cold SOBs in the winter! I'd see icebergs and the aurora borealis from the ship. We used to go real far north, up into Canada, and drop passengers off before going down to New York. We were practically at the Arctic Circle and would see these beautiful lights. I was just a kid: I didn't know what they were. I was scared. "What the hell is that? What's all these lights about? What's goin' on here?" Then somebody told me what they were.

It was a 5-day trip from Liverpool to New York. The refugees would travel 3rd class, in steerage, the ship's bottom rear end, which was so loud and uncomfortable even the crew wouldn't sleep there. It cost 'em about 10 quid, which would have been about $15 in those days, maybe a week's pay.

I was a server—serving the passengers while they ate and such. Our wages were sent home to our parents, but we all got a small allowance on the ship. And we'd make as much as $100 in tips after a 5-day run, which was plenty to keep us in trouble. We'd go to the crew bar where Guinness was 6 pence a pint. I'd have 5 pints a day.

So I was in New York with the ship, drinking lots of Guinness, at age 15.

Then our ship changed ports from Liverpool down to Southampton in southern England, and we'd do cruises down to the Mediterranean—sun, women.... We'd go to North Africa, and to Israel before the 1967 Arab-Israeli War. Back then Beirut was a safe place to go. It was called "The Paris of the Near East," and was such a beautiful city. It was on the old silk route to China. The Arab merchants there traded gold, silver, and jewels. I would buy forged guineas, the gold coins that were England's currency. They were very inexpensive in Beirut, and I'd bring them back to England and sell them in the pubs for profit.

As kids from Liverpool, anywhere was exotic. As soon as that ship docked, and we'd finished our duties, we were down that gangplank. There was a little gang of about 8 of us commie waiters or stewards, we were called. Busboys. We were all in one cabin, and we'd all hang out together. We'd steam down the gangplank and find a cab. In Beirut, North Africa, or Casablanca, we'd get a horse-drawn cab driven by a guy with a whip. We'd give him a couple of pennies, and a bag of salt that we'd stolen off the ship.

Back then, the mid-'60s, the desert countries didn't have easy access to salt, so it was valuable there. We'd just take it from the ship's stores, four 40-pound bags each, stuffed under our coats, and we'd all gang up real close together down the gangplank. A 40-pound bag of salt would pay for a night out: We'd give the taxi driver a bag of salt, and he'd drive us to the pyramids or wherever we wanted, there and back—he'd wait for us. It's an important commodity for everybody on the planet. You have to have salt in your body to live. But I only learned this later. I thought these guys were just using a lot of salt on their lamb and kebabs!

But of course everybody knew we were taking the salt—everybody had a scam going, from the Master at Arms on down. It was just the way things were done. Yeah, we had morals, and we'd kill for each other! But as far as makin' a profit, we weren't shy about thievin'. Every now and then I'd confess it to my priest. "God bless me, Father, for I have sinned. I robbed 4 bags of salt in Casablanca."

"Five 'Hail Mary's,' 2 'Our Father's.' Don't do it again!"

"Yes, sorry, I won't do it again."

It was wonderful. It was fabulous. We had a great time. And we got into trouble. Liverpool people are known for trading, making a deal, finding out a way to get something without really paying for it. It's clever, but it's also considered stealing! But within our group that's the way we thought; we thought we were being very smart bastards.

In Alexandria, Egypt, you could rent a moped for about 5 shillings a day, which is nothing. You didn't need a license, you'd just give them the money and they'd give you this little motorized bike. You'd scoot around, go see the sights, stop in the bars, and get around town better than you would trying to pay for taxis. We'd bring the mopeds back to the ship, go behind a crane or something and dismantle them. We'd take them on board under our coats—one person had a couple of wheels, someone else had the frame and the engine—and hide them. So that's more than "borrowing." We'd take the wheels off and have them under our bunks.

We'd get a moped back to Southampton. With customs you had to declare your stuff and pay tax on items of value you were importing. As you landed you had a little customs clearance ticket, and when you passed the gates of the docks to go out they had policemen standing there. You had to have this pass to go ashore. But what you did was put some money in the pass, gave it to the policeman, and whatever was in the taxi just went through. And with about 600 people out of a cruise ship landing, each giving the policeman a bit of money, a man could make quite a nice bonus. God bless the policemen. It doesn't happen anymore.

I was a gypsy. I got around a lot on the ships, but I only did it for about 2 years.

Then in 1966 the shipping industry went on strike for the usual reason: more money. I was down in Southampton, the southern port I used to sail from, out of work. What to do now? The strike looked like it was going to last a long time, and those ships weren't going to be moving.

One of the guys in my cabin said, "I know! Let's go down to Butlins!" Butlins is an English institution, a holiday camp. Billy Butlin had started holiday camps in the '30s, and during World War II the Army took over some of the camps for posts. After the War Butlin took over some Army posts and RAF bases—all the Nissen hut barracks, sheds, and things—for camps. He painted the buildings bright colors, planted gardens, refurbished the cafeterias, put in a couple of music halls, dug a hole in the ground and threw some cement and water in and called it a pool…it was pretty rough at best. You still lived in a Nissen hut, but you got out of the city. They'd have a little miniature golf course, dancing at night, pints of Guinness, beauty contests and dancing contests. They're a lot more sophisticated now.

Butlin was knighted by the Queen in 1964 for bring so much to the people. Thank God he was knighted, because he gave a lot of people an affordable opportunity to get out of the city. You could take a family there for a whole week for 10 quid—about a week's pay—and one price paid for everything, including all the activities and 3 meals a day. Except you'd have to buy your own beer and beverages. They'd have a dance hall and a 3rd-rate band, and the parents would dance. You could get away from inner-city life and spend time at a camp. It was like being on a cruise ship, only on land. You could get entertained for a week for a minimal amount of money.

My friend and I took the train down the coast to this place—they were always on the coast because people love to see the coast. England's an island, but if you're stuck in bloody downtown Birmingham in the middle of nowhere, you want to see the ocean.

They had a big cafeteria that could seat hundreds, if not a thousand, and we got jobs in the kitchen making up meals. It was the easiest job in the world because all the food was precooked. It came out of big steam ovens onto warm plates. There'd be a line of us guys, and a plate would slide in front of you. If you were on mashed potatoes, *dunk*, mashed potatoes, then you'd give it to the next guy. *Dunk*, meat. They could feed everyone for minimal cost.

At twelve o'clock we'd open the doors for lunch, and it'd be like a riot. Everyone wanted to sit down, everyone was hungry. The waitresses would take a rack of 8 plates from the ovens, all fully made up, and walk down the tables passing out meals like cards from a deck, throwing them in front of people. There was no class, no serving, just *dunk dunk*, "Here's your dinner, shut up, eat it." And there was no menu. What you got is what you 'et. But everyone loved it.

As workers we could fudge it and make anything we wanted. We were in a position to take advantage of the situation. As always.... It was a good job. They paid us, fed us, gave us a place to sleep. It was seasonal work, in the summer, otherwise it's too cold: When you're at the Atlantic, the camp's not gonna happen in the winter.

Back in Liverpool

About three-quarters into the season I got a phone call from my older sister Diane. My mum was in hospital with lung and brain cancer, and there wasn't anything they could do. They've got great medicine now, but in those days, it was, "Don't know. Here's some painkillers." You suffered. You died. My mother died, and I was back in Liverpool in the fall of 1966.

It was hard on me, yeah, but it was really hard on my sisters, God bless them, 'cause they still lived with her in a Council house, No. 1 Aspes Road, where rent was paid to the Liverpool City Council. It was subsidized, like the projects. When my mum died we were still a family, but the Council wanted to break us up because we had no parents. Diane was right on the edge of adulthood. She would be 18 that May. But legally they couldn't sign over the house to her, because the house belonged to the Liverpool City Council. And they didn't care who you were, they wanted you out the house.

My younger sister Susan would have gone to an orphanage, and Diane and I would have just been on the streets. But my older sister pled, battled with them, argued with them, and our aunts and uncles did loads of pleadin' too. A lot of people got involved in it. The Council relented in the end because it was a short time anyway before Diane turned 18, and let us stay at the house for the interim period, then Diane was officially the head of household.

If it wasn't for my sisters, God knows what would have happened to me. Maybe I'd have gone back into the Navy. Maybe find some trouble. But in retrospect, my mother's death got me in the music business.

This was roughly 1968 to 1969. I didn't own a record player, so whatever was on the radio, I listened to. There was a lot of good radio, and a lot of pirate radio as well.

Rock 'n' roll was just happening. The Beatles—from my hometown —were just becoming known. They really started around 1962 when Ringo joined. They'd come back from Germany and play in The Cavern, which was becoming famous.

American bands used to come over, like Percy Sledge, Martha and the Vandellas…you name them, they'd come to The Cavern. A lot of black bands used to come to Liverpool because they were fully accepted. Liverpool is a big port city full of everybody from everywhere, so there was no prejudice then. People didn't care where the music came from.

I worked behind the counter at a coffee shop, The Crooked Pot, which was just 2 doors from The Cavern. We used to get a lot of Cavern people in there, mainly artists. Gerry and the Pacemakers, The Beatles, and others would do lunchtime sessions at The Cavern, then it would close. A lot of people would just come over to the café I worked in and sit around for hours until The Cavern opened again. Everybody knew who was who. There was a big scene in Liverpool then with a lot of clubs, like The Jacaranda.

Prison for a Scooter Violation

In those days, I was a Mod. Go see The Who's movie *Quadrophenia* and you'll see what we were like. It's all about the 1960s Mods and the Rockers. I was a Mod. We dressed in little suits and ties, and shiny shoes, and little tight trousers. The Rockers were all bikers—leather and spitting, and we were all like, "Ah, bull to that."

We didn't ride motorbikes, we drove scooters. Mine was a 250cc Lambretta, and my engine columns were painted like the Union Jack. It had something like 32 mirrors.

My scooter actually belonged to my friend, but he had 2, and he let me borrow one. I didn't have a license, didn't have any insurance. I don't even think it was taxed. It was, "Ah, sod all that. That's just paperwork, who needs it."

And then one…fine…evening, I got stopped by the cops 'cause they noticed that it didn't have a disk. In England they have a little disk that shows you have insurance. I didn't have a license either. So they gave me a ticket.

I had to pay it and go to court and all that…which I totally ignored. I was like, "Ahh, okay, see you, pal," and just carried blithely on my merry way.

And about 6 months later there's a knock on the door, Aspes Road, where I was living with my sister Diane. It was 2 cops. "Right. You're under arrest. Son."

Ahh! "Why?"

"Because ya didn't pay yer dues."

They took me to jail! Two weeks! In Walton Prison. Walton Prison, in Liverpool, is…HEAVY! It's… murderers! Rapists! Killers! Gangsters, guns…! It's one of the heaviest prisons in Northern England. This prison's gates look like the gates of hell. I was scared to death! Two weeks in jail! I had my own cell, thank God. A tile cell. Every morning you had to get up and clean the floor, scrub it with your toothbrush. *Heavy* gig! Man.

At the very end of it, when I was ready to be released, these other prisoners said, "Yeah, you're only here for a piss and a shave, you little rat." To these guys, two weeks was bollocks! To me it was a lifetime.

Three days before I was due to be released, they were gonna let me out 'cause they needed my cell for somebody who'd probably just killed 12 people or something. So I was gettin' kicked out. And everybody'd 'eard about it, right?

That morning I came out my cell, and the other inmates grabbed me. I remember this vividly. They had steel brushes for scrapin' ironworks, and they…gouged me. My whole back, my shoulders, all over…. They scrubbed me with these brushes. And then threw red paint all over me. All because I was gettin' out, and I was a little rat, a little nobody. I was just in there for a *traffic* offense, for God's sake. These guys would cut people's hearts out.

Eventually the wardens come and get me, all casual. "Oh…. What happened to you?"

I said, "No. It didn't happen." You're not allowed to say anything, right? So they gave me bus fare to get home, and kicked me out. Took weeks for that stuff to come out my skin. Awww, yeah, lovely. It wasn't very pleasant.

The probation officers would come by to talk to me after I got back. "Ya learned yer lesson?"

"Yep. Yep, I did, that."

They have to come by, pro forma and pretend they're gonna turn you into an angel. They had to come 'round and fulfill the obligation, make sure I wasn't a threat to society.

I was riding a *scooter*, for God's sake. I wasn't killin' anyone. Oh, man. Two weeks in a high security jail for riding a bloody 250cc scooter…. Didn't pay the fine. Sorry! I CERTAINLY won't do it again.

First Roadie Gig: St. James Infirmary

So there I was in Liverpool when I was 18 and 19, just hanging around, not doing much of anything. I bumped into a friend I went to school with, Mark Clarke. He was a bass player in a local band called St. James Infirmary, after an old blues song from America. The guitarist—who was incredible—was really, really into blues, and he chose the name. They played pubs, workingmen's clubs. It was quite a nice little band. Mark asked if I would drive the truck, set up on stage, help with their amps, drive their little van. Be a roadie, that is. So I said, "Oh yeah, sounds like it'd be interesting."

He said, "We'll give you £5 a night, and a couple of pints of Guinness."

"Well, that's a deal." So off we went. They got successful within Liverpool.

A great guy, Kenny Smith, was one of the local boys. I didn't know him from school—he was 3 years older and a Protestant at that, so we'd gone to different schools. He'd come to the coffee shop; I'd see him in The Cavern. He was doing the same thing I was, but he had aspirations to be management. He saw an opportunity with St. James Infirmary, took over their management, and got them bigger shows.

We had a good time. But the van became too small after we built our own PA system. Kenny and I built huge speaker cabinets, like coffins: 8-foot-high single boxes with great big bass woofers. Bigger is better! We knew how to wire them, and Kenny was quite good with a saw and nails. We said, "We can make 'em!" Anyone can make a box and throw speakers in it. *Bang bang*, off we go. Plus speakers we'd robbed off of other bands, and a couple of amplifiers to drive it. It was difficult to move the stuff. Everybody had to help.

Kenny bought a bigger van, an ex-Army telecommunications field van painted bright yellow, like a yellow submarine. It had antennas, and was armor-plated—straight out the war. It had a great big steering wheel and was really high, with steps to get into it. And it had a crew cab—"Whoa, we're happenin'! A crew cab!" I'd grind the clutch, grind the clutch. There was no driver's license system, you just got in something and they told you how to do it, and off you went. Eventually some people took a test. I never did get a license.

The Beatles were moving along too. Since we were all from Liverpool, I understood what they were singing about. I understood their language—not meaning their accents, but where they were going with their songs, and what they were saying.

People from Liverpool always considered themselves the #1 Beatles fans. And when they had moved to London in 1962 there were riots in Liverpool! People were throwing bricks through record store windows, and on the phone to their MP (Member of Parliament) about it.

When The Beatles moved, Liverpool cried, "They've left us!" And there's always been a big competition in England. Liverpool is considered Northern, so if you're from there you're "Northern," meaning peasant. It was very insular as well. There are people who've never left Liverpool; there are people I know who've never left their neighborhood to go downtown Liverpool. I know people who would happily live on their street their entire lives, go to the local pub for entertainment, fish and chips for food, and the local corner store for the groceries. That's it. They don't even have telephones: They use public phones.

To me, someone leaving Liverpool wasn't a big deal because I'd been in the Merchant Navy and I'd already traveled a lot. So distances to me were just relative. Travel to London, big deal. But to the average Liverpool girl or guy, The Beatles might as well have gone to Mars.

Londoners had the museums, the arts, the cars, the houses. So it's like there was a line between the two cities…and now *they* got The Beatles. Their manager, Brian Epstein, had so much faith in them. And he wanted them to become famous throughout the world. And also rich.

That was it. We had lost The Beatles! I saw girls weeping openly in the streets. "We've lost them!" and "We'll never see them again!" But The Beatles were on the way: London one day, the next thing they've gotta conquer America! To a Liverpool band, London's just around the corner if you've got America in your sights.

In London and on Tour with Procol Harum

St. James Infirmary was a good band. They were getting bigger gigs, charging more, and Kenny was enjoying managing it, and he knew what was going on in the music scene in Liverpool. I was just the box pusher and etc. But it was a good team.

One day Kenny just said, "Right. We're going to London." We were like, "*Oh no*! What? What! Who?" Everybody in music wanted to go to London. I mean, London! You know, Rolling Stones, The Who, records, people, money…girls! It's all there.

"Yeah," Kenny said, "we're gonna go to London. We should do all right."

Then we're all thinking, "Record deals! We'll be on tour! We'll make money!" I'm thinking, "I'm gonna be a roadie for a *big* band!"

So we packed all our belongings, totally trusting, and put everything in our truck/radio van, the Yellow Submarine. This was about 1968, I think, when I was 19. It was me, Kenny, and the guys in the band: Mark Clarke on bass, Pete Rooney on drums (no relation), Dave Martin on guitar. We had our suitcases, all the equipment we owned. And off we went down the motorway for about 5 hours.

We got to London, and Kenny'd rented us a 1-room flat, which was …a joke. A kitchen and 1 room. I mean, it was horrible, filthy, dirty, just like the TV show *The Young Ones*: 6 guys living in this little flea pit, and, "That milk was mine in the fridge!" "Oh, no, that was my piece of cheese!"

St. James Infirmary played RAF and American Air Force bases in England and Germany. It wasn't really a tour—we'd try to put 5 gigs together down in Wales, over in Yorkshire, or in Germany. We used to do American Air Force bases because they liked the blues—a lot of black people. We played at Ramstein Air Force Base in Germany. Great base, actually. It's like an American city. We used to go to the BXs and buy all sorts of crap.

We hardly had any income, except for Kenny. And if there was some work, they put me on the crew just to give me some cash. I'd go help out on gigs around London for a couple of pints in the pub here and there. Kenny was helping out with The Cream's bassist Jack Bruce's solo project fusion band, Lifetime, with drummer Tony Williams, guitarist John McLaughlin, and Larry Young playing the Hammond organ. Their road manager, Bob Adcock, was a good friend of Kenny's, and would give Kenny some extra work while St. James Infirmary were getting ourselves organized with agents to book us, and trying to do some local shows.

I was on the crew at The Albert Hall when The Cream played their final shows, November 25 and 26, 1968. Had to look that date up—I didn't even know what year it was myself sometimes. That was one of those gigs when a couple of me mates called me to help, to do some lifting and pushing at The Albert Hall, for The Cream.

I didn't really know Ginger Baker other than I said "Hello" to him, that kinda thing. He was a total lunatic. He's the guy who went to Africa and lived in the bloody bush, with the nomads. He just disappeared. "Anyone seen…?" He used to be in the clubs, hanging out and that, and all of the sudden it's like, "Hey, you haven't seen Ginger, have ya?" "Haven't seen him, no." The next thing ya know, it's in the newspapers. He flew to bloody North Africa one time, got in a Jeep or something, and just disappeared out into the Atlas Mountains, 'cause he'd heard there was some great native drummers. Right? And he just disappeared. For 7 or 8 months he lived in Africa with these nomads, ridin' camels around from camp to camp and stuff. Crazy bastard!

Anyway, that's how I learned what the equipment was doing, how it plugged in, what kinda sound system and microphone was what. And I was learning with very good people, like Ginger Baker—with the craziest drum kit in the world!—and you have to learn how to mike that off. And how to mike it in stereo, because things were just going into stereo then.

So I was in, but I wasn't on payroll. If you were on payroll, even when you weren't on the road touring, the management would give you 20 quid of subsistence money a week, a retainer, just to keep you. If they had a good crew, they didn't want you to just disappear on them. Then they could use you around town, driving equipment from here to there, one studio to another, rehearsals. They'd keep you busy. Then when you were on the road you'd make about £100 maximum per week, which was quite a lot of money in those days. Plus your keep—hotel and lodging, and a per diem of about £10 for living expenses. As for the band members, let's say Procol Harum when we were the opening act with Ten Years After and Jimi Hendrix, the band members would make a couple grand a week each.

The bands then were all mind-melding. Everybody was playing with everybody else—Cat Stevens, The Beatles, The Who. There was always a bit of work, and I got to know all the roadies. And they'd go, "Oh, yeah, Bryan was all right," and they'd give me £20, and buy me a couple pints of Guinness. They'd be shorthanded or doing an extra special gig, or only have X amount of hours to put it together, they'd go "Bryan could do that" and they'd call me. I was kind of a freelance apprentice roadie. It was a good learning experience.

In fact the job of roadie was invented then. I mean, nobody'd ever done this. Nobody knew what a roadie was. The job didn't exist until then. We invented the job, because the bands couldn't set up their own gear in front of 5,000 people, God bless 'em. Part of the job was protectting the band—there were some heavy lads in the crews. Roadies are like marauding Vikings, just hooligans really, a closed society of…thugs! The road crews are ruthless. They don't give a monkey's wedding about anybody or anything. They're hard-workin', hard-drivin', hard-drinkin', hard-playin' guys. And we'd all help each other out. If somebody was in trouble, there'd be 20 roadies on your case with brass knuckles.

We had a lot of fun because we were with the band! "Hey, girl, I just did a show with The Cream…. What're you doing tonight?" Girls would sit next to you. Back when I was just a ship steward, not many girls would sit next to me in the pub or in a club, because I didn't have enough cachet. Which, for a Liverpool girl, is a bit pushing it, isn't it? The place is full of sailors, so half the time you're gonna be sitting next to 'em. What are you gonna do? Being a roadie in London gave you an in to a better social life, or at least a bigger one.

And there was always a party somewhere among the road crews. They'd just get back in from 6 weeks of slogging 'round Europe, and after getting their wages and per diems they'd have a fair amount of money when they came back to London. And when they were off the road, it was party time! "Where's the wife?" "Where's the girlfriend?" "Where's the parrot?" Whatever was going on! Everybody would just say, "Yeah, there's a party over at Ten Years After's sound engineer's house."

I enjoyed it. I mean, I'd been around a lot with the Merchant Navy—New York, Casablanca. I wasn't shy. It was, "Ahh, this is nice. Where's tonight's party?" And they'd have a big bathtub full of…whatever, and you drank it, and went home. Everybody was in the same place, the road crews.

Some nights I'd get a gig, or if I had some cash, I'd go to King's Road and just sit and listen to the music, have a drink, talk to the dolly birds—the little cute girls around the pubs. It was the '60s, you know: Carnaby Street, miniskirts…just like in *Austin Powers*. That was a whole scene, Carnaby Street and King's Road. I was still a Mod in those days, all dressed in button-down shirts…a *tie*, even! Hipsters, meaning low-slung trousers. In tartan. Scooters were all the rage. A lot of people did acid… "Yeah, groovy!" I never did. I didn't like losing my mind that much. Twelve pints of Guinness…now that was me.

But you had to know the right pub to be in, had to know where the people were gonna be going that night. I always knew. You could pretty much guarantee running into the same people on a nightly basis or on the weekend.

The first time I saw a musician and went, "Wow!" was Rod Stewart, at a club called The Marquee in the West End of London when he was just starting out. Rod the Mod. I thought, "This guy's good. He's really, really raw," and he had a great band.

The Marquee was a big club with a big dance floor. They used to have jazz and blues and stuff, then realized rock 'n' roll was moving along. So the guy who owned it, Jack Barry, God bless him, switched the club from blues and jazz to pop/rock. David Bowie would be there one night, then Peter Noone of Herman's Hermits, Elton John, The Small Faces. They all used to play at The Marquee. There was just a constant scene. Every night there was something different.

The Beatles were doing very well, thank you, so they weren't doing the clubs. They opened The Beatles Store on Baker Street about 1967, their psychedelic store and clothing company. It was a *big* hangout, and there was a pub next to it that had coffee. The store had all these clothes designed by a Swedish guy, of all people, very avant-garde. And they painted the whole building like a bubble, with the ball and stars and the moon and the sun. So we all hung out at this huge psychedelic building and would go to the pub next door, The Sherlock Holmes. 22½ Baker Street was where Sherlock Holmes lived in the books.

On occasions you'd see somebody like Paul or George go into the store. There was always enough people around to mob them. And if there wasn't, if one person saw a Beatle, within 5 minutes there'd be 30 people.

It was a big time. The clubs were raging—and I don't mean just the music clubs. The artists would be in the private clubs drinking and eating. There were some great restaurants in these clubs. And the clubs now had the power and the money that they wouldn't let you in if you didn't have a *lot* of money. Private clubs in London are *very* private.

And then all of the sudden this big thing happened: Peter Sellers, who was a member of all the clubs, got involved with them. Dudley Moore, his partner Peter Cooke, and a lot of those people liked what was happening, and they just gravitated around The Beatles, The Stones, The

Who. It was the thing to do. You'd go into a club and there'd be a table with Richard Burton, Elizabeth Taylor, Ringo, Rod Stewart, and somebody else. Name a band—The Cream, Jimi Hendrix, Zeppelin—they were all rolling through the same places.

All the big record labels were signing people to 5-year contracts: Decca, EMI, Polygram, Chrysalis, Island, and all the big American ones. Ever since somebody turned down The Beatles (who ended up under Capitol), everybody was scared they were gonna turn down the next Beatles. The fuckin' stupid suits! They were like, "You can play a guitar? Here, sign this contract!" The old companies had been turning out jazz, classical music, the spoken word. And all of the sudden somebody's making a coupla million pounds over here with this new stuff. "Oh…we've got studios…." They'd hire younger people who supposedly had half a clue as to what was going on. These guys suddenly have a company car, and their own live-in secretary. But half of them had no more clue than Adam. They were useless! But that's the name of the game, isn't it? The record company fuddy-duddies at "Cobweb Record Company" didn't know what was going on. Nobody really understood what was going on. Nobody! Even, God bless 'im, Brian Epstein. His idea of clean and neat was suits, so he put The Beatles in suits and cleaned 'em up, thought that's what the people would want. And he was right. He made it up as he went along—and he made the right decisions. Epstein put it together.

But unfortunately, nothing happened for the band I was with, St. James Infirmary. Kenny just couldn't get a deal for them. They couldn't get signed because they were playing the wrong stuff: blues. The labels wanted pop, Beatles, The Rolling Stones, anti-establishment stuff, crazy teenage rebel stuff from the hell. "Get on your scooter, pop some pills, and crash" was the name of the game for the record store customers and concert audiences.

The BBC had *Ready Steady Go*, which was *the* show to watch, the weekly *have*-to-watch-it pop show. It was a precursor to *The Old Gray Whistle Stop*, like *The Ed Sullivan Show* became in America. They got all the top bands on the show because the bands got great exposure on it.

St. James Infirmary just didn't have it. They tried to adjust, and Kenny tried. They're named after an old blues song, so they were obviously blues-based, and very good, but things were moving away from blues at that time, toward "love, love me do." They didn't have that—it wasn't in them. St. James Infirmary was more into playing their instruments, being bloody musicians, as opposed to being songwriters. Kenny tried to push 'em in that direction, nudge 'em, but it just never worked, which is a shame because they were brilliant musicians, all of them. The drummer, Peter Rooney, was fabulous. Mark Clarke the bass player eventually ended up with a really big time blues band, Jon Hiseman's Colosseum, which were very, very big in Europe. And in fact he's back with them now, 2006! Dave Martin was brilliant. You could hold him up to Eric Clapton. But they just fell apart, and we were all on our own.

One of Two Roadies for Procol Harum

So there I was in London, robbing milk off the doorsteps.

I didn't have a dime, really. I was earning spot money for a while, about a year. Maybe I could afford to go into a club once, twice a week if it was a good week. The rest of the time I had to eat. I rented a room with a bed, a little 1-room thing with an electric heater to boil a kettle to make tea. And that was it, that's all I could afford.

I could still go in most places because I knew the bouncers, the doormen, who'd go, "Ahh, come on, in you go." I'd get in there and maybe have enough money for ½ pint, then that was it. I could sit there like an idiot…unless one of the guys would buy me a drink. Then I'd get the Tube home.

And then one night, in 1970 I believe, I was over at a club, The Marquee, talking to the boys and all that, looking for work. A blond guy goes, "Oh, you should speak to Mike, he's looking for somebody."

"Who's Mike with?"

"Procol Harum."

I found Mike, and said "I heard you're looking for 1 or 2 people."

He said, "Oh yeah. You've been here before. You'll do. I haven't got enough money for anybody else, but the 2 of us can do it." That was the interview. Imagine that, take a band on the road with 2 guys! Do all the drivin', set everything up, do the gig, take it all down, drive another 500 kilometers, get 4 hours sleep, do it again.

So I said, "Well, okay, great."

"All right. Come over to Chrysalis Records tomorrow, and I'll put you on payroll." Oh, *yeah*! I'm gonna get steady money on a weekly basis! It would be about £20 a week in town.

So next day I go over to Chrysalis on Oxford Street in the West End, and Procol Harum are rehearsing for a tour. Mike and I go down to the rehearsal hall at Shepherd's Bush, an area of London about 8 miles away. They had already made a deal with High Watt and were expecting a whole truckload of amplifiers and cabinets any minute. High Watt were a new company about 30 miles north of London. They were giving out equipment left and right at cost to get it on stage and on television. Everybody else, like The Who, had Marshalls; High Watts were knock-offs of Marshalls, tube amps.

It was great equipment. It was built well, built for the road, heavy. That's important 'cause the amplifiers got the shit beat out of them, especially in those days. They'd bounce down a flight of stairs, get kicked, beer thrown at them or poured in them. You threw the stuff. But the guitars and drums were—are—treated like gold, like babies. You'd be in trouble if you turned up with a Les Paul with a broken neck. But I knew how to fix amplifiers: They were just tube amps, and you'd just replace tubes. It wasn't like today's state-of-the art equipment. It was an amplifier for God's sake. In a coupla weeks its all shredded, patched up, a bit of tape here. Today it's all flight cases and padding.

So anyway Mike and I went out to High Watt, which took about an hour in our truck. We signed for the equipment, loaded the truck up, loaded the truck some more, and then took it back and set everything up in the rehearsal studio.

Mike was doing the sound for them. He was into it. They had a WEM sound system—*big*, with column speakers, and you could scale it up as you went along. That was the technology: The bigger, the louder, the better. They had slave amps, and you slaved amp to amp to amp from here to wherever you wanted to go. You had to know what the hall was capable of taking, the breakers, and adjust your amps to the incoming power.

We first went to tour Germany. Then we went everywhere—France, Norway, Sweden, all fabulous places. You'd drive your truck onto the car ferry to Sweden in the middle of winter, and by the time you'd get to Sweden, you're seriously seasick from The North Sea.

Mike and I took care of the stage equipment—amplifiers, organs, drums, keyboards—carting them around *all* by manpower. And things weren't really organized, 'cause nobody knew how touring was supposed to work. We're going to go do 6 weeks in Germany. And a lot of it's gonna be really hard schlepping up stairs, because you're gonna be doing a gig in a beer house and you've gotta get all this stuff set up. Hammond organs are huge, and a Leslie cabinet is so big it needs 4 men to lift it— and we had 6 of them! And you've gotta get up those stairs. There's no union involved. The promoters were supposed to supply bodies to help ya, but on a lot of occasions they'd try to *not* get people to help, because they'd have to pay each body, each German, 100 Deutschmarks, 20 or 30 bucks. They didn't want to pay it, the cheap bastards.

Train Tour with Jimi Hendrix and the Grateful Dead

During that time Kenny was working with Bob Adcock, tour manager for Jack Bruce's band Lifetime. He had it much more together. I was like a jackrabbit. I literally sometimes didn't know what month it was— and I didn't care. I didn't even have a watch.

Procol Harum made a fair amount of money touring Europe. We used to open for Ten Years After. We did some amazing things, like the train tour with Jimi Hendrix, Ten Years After, Procol Harum, and the Grateful Dead, all on one train. I think it was still 1970…?

It was a party train. Girls…women…drugs, it's all there: marijuana, hashish. They'd be smoking the coal from the engine if they had the choice. All the way to the back where the conductor was there were naked women…! Ah, flashbacks! And then at each main stop we had to get off the train, get our equipment off the boxcars, hope the promoter's turned up with enough trucks for all these groups' equipment, and get it over the gig, wherever that might be.

We were working off the seat of our pants. We didn't really know how to tour because nobody had really toured with 6 bands, 6 drum kits. There was a huge amount of learning—for everyone, including the bands. But we all had a great time. We all got hotels, got fed, got per diems. Good times.

Because Procol Harum were the opening act, we were the last ones to set up but the first ones to play, so we had about 6 feet of stage, with all the other bands' equipment racked up behind us. But after a while everybody knew what they were doing, knew the system. Like there's no point in everyone trying to get stuff off stage left when you can get stuff off left and right. And so whatever gig we went to, we kind of invented it as we went along. There was no super roadie who had it all planned out for us.

I knew every band's plectrums, their picks. "Plectrum" sounds much more sophisticated, doesn't it? I was the guy who invented taping the picks to the mike stand. I put double-looped gaffer tape on the mike stand for the guitarist for Procol Harum. One night he came out on stage and was playin', and playin', and he's lookin' at this thing on his mic stand. Then he loses his plec… and it's "Ah! It's fuckin' brilliant!" Bought me a pint for that. I did it one night and next thing you know all the other roadies were doing it. We were living it.

And we knew each other and what each other's band had. Hendrix's guy wouldn't hesitate to give me an amp or vice versa. It doesn't matter, 'cause our job was to get these people on stage, make 'em sound good, look good.

In those days lighting was very basic: a coupla stands with a coupla cord lights, and that was it. No mixers or anything. Nowadays you have *days* to set up, and sound checks, and camera checks. And nowadays it's not so much freelancers and gypsies.

For us, you'd maybe have a sound check 15 minutes before, if you were lucky. You might be playing in a 10,000 seat bicycle racing stadium in France. You can imagine the acoustics ain't too good! It was like playin' in a bathroom. The sound would just bounce everywhere. So there would be a wooden track, banked, and you'd build the stage at one end, stick a bunch of seats in the middle, and there's your gig, thank you very much. "Oh, here's a light."

Even the power was a bit awkward because English equipment is totally different power-wise—different voltage, that is. So you'd have to have a lot of transformers. We learned not to trust anyone to bring them, but to carry our own. We'd buy them in England or Germany or wherever and have them shipped to us, then we would carry all our own adapters and transformers in our trucks with us. You could never rely on somebody else to have the right equipment for you: You had to be self-sufficient. But it was just another step, another level of work, that had to be done.

You try and set your equipment to optimize the space you're in, to at least not make it sound like the public baths in Brighton which would be just one big echo. You try and set the equipment so that the people in the 50th row could hear what the people on stage were saying or singing. Today's equipment is so sophisticated, it could probably hit you itself. In those days it was literally on, off, bass, treble. Your radio had more controls. But what did we know? Off we went, and we were the roadies! "Oh, yeah, we're cool."

As for my hearing, we'd be behind the stage, stage left or right, with the speakers directed toward the audience. So that's probably why my hearing is okay: We were behind the speakers. Not that I thought in those terms then. Although we were quite clever in those days, not just a bunch of ignorant bastards. We actually thought about things.

So you'd set all that in your 15 minutes or so before the show started, and then sometimes the artists would stroll on stage, plug in their guitars, go, "Brang! *Brang!*" adjust something and say, "Oh, that's better."

They were *never* loud enough. And then they'd go up to the mike, "Eee, eeek," squeal, howl…it would drive you crazy.

Jimi Hendrix was one who would adjust things by cranking them as high as they would go. But you can't blame them, 'cause with 15 minutes or less of setup, the roadies often didn't have enough time to get it right before the band went on.

Watching Hendrix play was amazing, 'cause nobody had seen anything like it. You just hadn't. Nobody had. And he came from America—"Jimi Hendrix? Who the heck is that? What are you talking about?" He first played at The Speakeasy in 1969, one of *the* places to be. It was one of the first clubs catering to rock music, the roadies, and the bands, and who was who in the business was there. They had a doorman. If you weren't with *somebody*, you weren't getting in. It was semiprivate, so it wasn't full of little dolly birds fallin' all over the place. And it had great food. Their a restaurant was walled off with glass so you could eat without getting your ears blown out. So Jimi got on stage and started playing, and I think Clapton's sitting there, The Who's over here, and Ringo's there. And this black guy from America—with all this hair—starts all this, and everyone's going "What *is* that? What's *that* all about?" He was what he was. He freaked people out! And he changed a lot of stuff.

We were lucky on that particular train tour that everyone got along. Pretty much everyone knew what was supposed to happen, and the best way to do that was to just get on with it. I've seen some bad maneuvers on other tours, like if somebody didn't like somebody they'd put a mike stand through his Les Paul, just because he said something wrong on the bus. These are rough people. Some of these musicians are straight out of jail. But this train tour wasn't like that.

A lot of people then were just independent-minded. To do music, wear hippie clothes, to do more music, to have an afro, you have to be independent. You had to have a different way of looking at it at first, before it became commercial. When a guy could walk down Carnaby Street with 6-inch heels on, you had to be different anyway.

Even the road crews had their own little niche, and we had our own hierarchy, our own language. You know who is what, why, where, who's doing what to why and how. The road crews didn't really hang out with the bands. It's bad for your image—the road crew's image, not the band's. The bands were too busy, of course, with interviews, rehearsals, recording. And we're too busy too, with no lives, driving 36 hours non-stop to the next gig. Oh, the pills we had to pop…. Road crews are like lumberjacks. We hung out with each other: It was sissy to hang out with the bands.

So that was our environment. As I said earlier, it hadn't been done before. You take 6 bands on the road with people going, "What's an amplifier?" And you're trying to get yourself organized. Then you go and do it and you come back with more experience. And then you can tell your buddies, "Oh, we did this," and "This is a good way to mike up this," and "If you do this, you get this effect."

And the artists did the same thing: sharing, playing, hanging out. There wasn't this rivalry going on between Eric Clapton and Jimi Hendrix and Jimmy Paige. They respected each other, and knew each other's capabilities. There might have been a little bit of, "Oh, he's got a bigger amp than me," but I don't think it really kept them awake at night. It was more, "Hi Jimi!" "Hi Eric!" Even after being on tour you'd see the artists back in the clubs because they were comfortable. The Speakeasy had a little stage and they'd just wander in, and whoever was there got on the stage and off they went for 1 or 2 songs, then they'd go and have dinner. Sometimes Hendrix, Paige, and Clapton were all on The Speakeasy stage together, maybe play some of each. Everyone was really comfortable—no hustle, no hassle, no pressure. It was good fun, very cool.

Also, everybody was fighting against the same thing, which was the government. And the government—Harold Wilson was Prime Minister, with the Labor Party—the government was *not* amused with kids running around the streets saying, "Peace! Love!" That's where it started.

The Isle of Wight Festival

Procol Harum did the Isle of Wight Festival on this little island in the bloody English Channel, from August 26-30, 1970, about a year after

Woodstock. It was hysterical. It was great. Name a band of the era, and they were there: Hendrix, Ten Years After, Peter Frampton, Joan Baez, Chicago, Miles Davis, The Doors, Jethro Tull, Tiny Tim, Moody Blues, Supertramp, Joni Mitchell, Sly and The Family Stone, The Who. Everybody was there: 80,000 people, maybe 250,000.

By then everybody actually knew what they were doing, which did help, especially when it came to projecting the sound. It was getting professsional. In general the gigs had bigger crowds, and bigger and more sophisticated equipment, because the bands wanted people to hear them. Why go through all this drama and hassle of putting this *huge* show together if only the people in the first 5 rows can hear it? It was all part of the gig.

I go into the Chrysalis office, and they tell me, "We're doing a show, *big* show. The Isle of Wight. Get our equipment together, rent the truck. You go in the day before we're playing. Just get down there, set it up."

I had 15 days. "Oh, okay, no problem. Give me a map," I said.

Then a couple days later, they said, "We've got a truck rented for ya, and you're on the last boat today to the Isle of Wight."

"Oh, okay, so I'd better get moving." I drove like a maniac in a 10-ton truck, brrrrrrrrrmmm, with all the equipment. Nowadays a 10-ton is nothing: People travel with 18-wheelers. So a 10-ton truck was more like a vegetable delivery van. But Mike and I got everything in it, and off we went, yo! On our merry way, two little dudes. I mean, I was small, but Mike was like a troll. Two small guys.

We get on the island, and the traffic—as per usual—is just totally nonsense. There was thousands and thousands of people walking down the streets and getting their camps set up—like Woodstock. It was *the* thing, the *big* thing.

Isle of Wight is a very posh part of England. I mean exclusive, and million-dollar homes. Writers and artists go to the Isle of Wight to work. And then in come thousands and thousands of people from all over England and Europe—Germany, Holland, Greece, France, everywhere.

I don't think all the locals were completely amused.... But generally speaking, everybody was welcomed. They were puzzled as well, "they" being the older people in England, generally speaking, and the Isle of Wight in particular, because they were retired rich people. They'd earned their money, settled, and were just…puzzled at what was happening.

There was a huge stage. We're talking about on-ramps, off-ramps, and the backstage was just huge.

Procol Harum really hit it. I mean, "Whiter Shade of Pale" will break your heart when you've got it "at 11" and everybody's out there going, "YEAHHHHHH!" Thousands of people were dancing to it, knew the music, sang the words. "Whiter Shade of Pale" was—and still is—a beautiful song. And they did brilliantly with it. Chrysalis Records were very happy.

Jimi Hendrix was his usual self: "Anyone got any lighter fluid?" Zzzzzp, bang, off we go, Jimi's happy. They carried crates of lighter fluid in their truck.

It was somewhat similar to Woodstock as far as some great bands, the mood, the free love, the drugs. But it was under control in terms of it didn't flood, there was not hundreds of people ODing, the bathrooms worked, there was a good phone system. The producers who put it together were very, *very* good. They knew what made a disaster, and they were determined to avoid it.

The producers wanted to make the festival happen every year, so they knew if they did it right, all the councils, permits, police, coast guard, and the ferry system would be a lot more conducive to help them. 1970 was actually the 3rd festival, following ones in '68 and '69.

But they couldn't get it together for the next one. Two years from then different bands didn't exist, some people were dead, a lot of people had come to America. It would have been a heavy gig to put together.

Frisian Islands Riot

Then Procol Harum went back to Germany and did another tour. Everybody is into festivals: "Right, you've done Woodstock…. Isle of Wight…," so the Germans wanted a piece of the action. Everybody thought, "Let's do a festival. We'll make money! All we have to do is find a farm, throw on some bathrooms and a big plank stage, and we'll charge everybody 20 Deutschmarks. We're rich!"

There was support coming from the labels, and the promoters in Germany wanted money. And the people wanted the bands. If you put a poster up: "Jimi Hendrix is appearing in a farm field 50 kilometers that way," a million people are gonna be there.

So this Frisian Islands gig was another Isle of Wight, but in Germany, north of Hamburg in the Zuider Zee between Germany and Sweden. Cold! Cold as cold could be. A train line went over a causeway to the island, so you didn't have to deal with ferries and shipping and traffic. You could drive to the island on the causeway too.

You don't know what a gig's gonna be before you get there. You look at a map, and it doesn't tell you. You just get there and see what's gonna happen.

Mike and I got to the hotel, and it was pouring rain. It rained and rained for 3 days before the show, then rained the show out. There was no setup time, and nobody's gonna put their equipment up in the rain when there wasn't even a roof. Procol Harum arrived, everybody else's people get in, and the hotel is just full. There's 50 floors full of lunatic English people with nowhere to go and nothing to do. Imagine....

The Germans—the fans—burned down the stage and the sound system with Molotov cocktails. It was over. They know how to do a riot in Germany. But I wasn't concerned: I was in the hotel with some of the hardest people from England!

Rockin' and Rollin' to Berlin

I was always arrogant enough to go, "I've got a tour, I've got a hotel, I get paid more than you." I guess that's arrogant, yeah. Even though my "office" was the front seat of a 10-ton truck, or whatever truck it was, with my partner Mike, passports, visas.

The only thing that nearly intimidated me was being at the checkpoints leaving West Germany to drive through East Germany to Berlin. Back then driving to Berlin through the middle of East Germany was a lot of hassle. There were submachine guns and paperwork, and in addition to East and West German control, there's American control, English control, and French control. And each one wants a different set of papers, and it all has to coincide with what you've got in your truck. We had to unload it over and over. They opened everything.

Then you're just driving down a 2-lane highway, the E-6, and there's a guard tower every mile or so on the road all the way, with soldiers and guns. You'd all stop at the same local café 'cause you're only allowed to stop at specific places on this particular road. There was pressure from the tension, the hair triggers, the rockets lined up toward each other's cities.

When you get to the other end of the E-6, there's more barbed wire, land mine fields, signs and people that say, "*Achtung!*" This is serious. And you're just trying to get into Berlin to entertain some poor buggers who haven't heard a decent band in a couple of months.

So then after a certain amount of hassles it became, "Sod these East Germans! We're gonna get it through! Yes, we can do it!" We were never scared, never worried, we just cruised. The rule was: Get there. It's like an army maneuver, or a naval or SAS (Special Air Services)—a lot of pressure. The trick is to get to the address on your book.

The Berlin show was at the Deutschlandhalle, like a town hall, with 2,000-3,000 people. It was Procol Harum, Ten Years After, and Canned Heat. Wherever people bought records, we went. Procol Harum was in the record stores, on the radio, in the teen magazines. They were being well promoted in Germany. This was September 4, 1970.

Fired from Procol Harum by Chrysalis

So Procol Harum played Berlin, opening for another Chrysalis Records band, Ten Years After. As their roadie I know every song in the show, every single guitar plink-plunk.

Then I was driving to the next show, somewhere in northern Germany. It was bleeding freezing. The truck, bump bang, stops in the middle of *Strassenfrasse Nickenbicken*…"Where am I?" I don't know. I'm in the middle of Germany and the truck's crapped out.

I had to walk about 5 miles before I found a goddamn pay phone to get through to Hertz, who we were renting the truck from. "Where are you?" they asked.

"I'm in Germany."

"No, where are you in Germany?"

"Okay, right." I found out, and we finally get it together, and they send a tow truck.

When the tow truck arrived, I've got my map, and I said, "Look, I *have* to be *here*," and I pointed 'cause I didn't speak German, "NOW."

And the guy said, "*Was? Was ist los?*"

"Tow me *here*." Fortunately it was only about 2 towns up the Autobahn. I'm already late. I should have been *at* the gig when this whole drama came down. The place holds about 5,000 and it was going to be packed because it had sold out. Anything English sold out. You know, it could have been "The Muppets in English" and it would have sold. (Is Frank Oz gonna have a go at me for saying that?) I know what the mood's gonna be. I *have* to get there, 'cause the show's got to go on.

So I get the truck towed to the show, and I'm shaking with nerves, "Oh…God." I run up 3 levels of stairs to where the actual concert is taking place. I get up on stage. Ten Years After are all set up, they're ready. The crowd is getting angry. But the management won't let Ten Years After do anything because we're the opening act.

We start schlepping and sweating this stuff up the flights of stairs. The promoter's finally cracked and he's paying some kids out the audience to come and help. It's all about Deutschmarks, isn't it?

Finally it's all up there, and I'm settin' up fast as I can. Well…it was getting a bit tense. One of the Chrysalis Records managers goes to a microphone and goes, "His fault! Him! HIM!"

I'm like, "What? What're we doing?"

The audience of 5,000 is screamin' and dancing around and getting really upset about it, throwing stuff at me as I'm dying trying to get this stuff on stage. This was *not* a nice thing for the manager to do, because

I've done *my* best. Any roadie would. You'd put yourself through anything: You'd jump over a barbed wire fence to get the gig going, walk through a minefield to do the show. It was embedded in us. We had dirty fingernails—we worked for a living.

The suits were there too, from Chrysalis. As I told you, nobody really knew what was going on in these tours except the road crew. You've got these guys in suits, "Look at me, I work for…." And to them, we were just scum with dirty fingernails. We had to work for our bloody money. And we *sweated*. But we were there to make this lot look and sound good. Those guys in the suits shouldn't have even been there, it was just something else to do on their expense account, to meet a coupla *fräuleins*.

Procol Harum were down in their dressing room, as usual. If anything major went wrong, like it did this particular night, they turned their backs on the whole situation and let this…idiot…from Chrysalis Records deal with it.

In those days, if we had any trouble on tour, it was the inflated, bloated, record company executives who handled it—with their nice suits, their Jaguars and dolly birds and their club memberships, scootin' around London like they owned it, makin' all the money while the artists and roadies are killin' themselves to have enough to eat. Fine. But don't get on the stage in front of me and accuse ME of being slack. I just nearly killed myself to get there.

So I'm trying to get the show working, and I'm getting soda cans and crap and all this stuff thrown at me—and German beer bottles are quite heavy. The guy's blaming me. I didn't build the truck! The excuses could go on and on, but if the truck breaks down, you do what you can to get on the road. You don't just sit there and twiddle your thumbs. I got on the road. I got it towed 60 kilometers. I got the equipment to the gig.

I'm laying cable, and one more time this Chrysalis bastard manager comes on stage and he's trying to apologize to the audience. He doesn't speak a word of German, so he's pointing at me and screaming, "It's HIS fault!"

His back is to the audience and he's screaming at me. He didn't realize, or forgot about, the 6-foot drop to the orchestra pit. At that point I just, well, I went "Sorry…" and I just sort of gently pushed him into the pit. Where he promptly broke a leg. "Sorry, I'm layin' a cable here, oops!" He was in my way. Well, okay…I knew what I was doing. If I'd lifted him up first it would've been another 2 feet to fall, and he might have fell on his back, which might have really hurt. It was just a casual push. He was trying to catch himself and the legs went first, and he broke one.

Note that I don't advise doing this.

Well, that calmed the crowd down. They thought it was hysterical. That took the onus off me, and I just carried on with my cabling and setup.

The guy in the pit screamed, "YOU'RE FIRED, YOU…[this, that, and the other]." I said, "Fine" and left the stage. I wanted out. I didn't come here to be a slave, and accused in front of 5,000 Germans of being an idiot, have stuff thrown at me.

By this time the band heard about it as it'd finally filtered down to the dressing rooms 3 floors below. Keyboardist Gary Booker was the band's chief—brilliant guy, great writer. He's like, "What's going on? I heard…."

I said, "Well, I've been fired. Here's the key to the truck." I still had my floater, that's my expense money, and my per diems. "Have a nice time."

I went out to the hotel that was booked for us, the Holiday Inn on the, um, *Ringenstadtendstunde*, wherever it was. Every German town has a *Ringstunde*, and you always stay in the Holiday Inn. My expense money was a couple hundred pounds for dramas, new cabling, amps. Tow truck. So I went to the Holiday Inn, had some good German beer and schnapps, went to bed with my conscience clear. I'd just had enough. So I went.

Next morning I got a train to the next major town, I think it was Hanover, and got a flight back to London.

Went to the Chrysalis office and…"You're fired."

It was the record executives who were making the money, and also there were some nasty managers. Everybody was out for themselves. You didn't see these guys buying me a pint of beer when I was schlepping boxes and tons of equipment, or offering to buy me a meal. They never did that. At least I never saw it. And you know what? Half the goddamn roadies in England will agree with me on that.

These days it's far too serious to mess with the crew; the management treats the crew like gold. If you're gonna be putting on Pink Floyd, you're not gonna treat your crew badly. If you've got a good crew, and you want your band to sound great, you don't wanna lose them. You're gonna go outta your way to keep the bastards happy. It only takes one or two guys to go, "See ya" and walk away for the tour to be in serious trouble. I've seen it happen. Then the managers have to go back to their record company bosses and explain it.

Back then there was a big shakeup on the way. I didn't cause it, but a lot of people just said, "Hey, whoa, hang on, we need more of the money we're making for the companies." The artists, the road managers, and the crews started going, "I can't even afford to go on the road because these people won't pay me. I'm gonna stay at home with my kids."

And if you've got a really talented piano roadie who can make you sound wicked and really nice on the piano, when some bloated executive fires him you're gonna go, "Hang on a minute!"

The drummers especially really want things *exactly* one way. Otherwise, when they're playing, if the goddamn cymbal's a ½ inch that way, they miss. And they're gonna throw it at you. So drum roadies are in charge of the kit, and the drummer's not going to spend an hour on stage under test lights and sound checks trying to put his own drum kit together.

From the light setup to the stage setup to the drum setup, the guys behind the scenes, the backstage personnel, are just as much a part of why these bands are so powerful. And there's some pretty spectacular shows going on out there these days. You've got 10 semis full of equipment versus the little yellow army telecommunications van St. James Infirmary had.

There's still a bunch of us hanging on, you know. A lot of them have died, God bless 'em. Bobby Reid, head carpenter for Elton John, is called "the old man" now, working with all these young guys who don't have a clue.

Germany: Touring with Reinhard Mey

So after my run-in with the suit from Chrysalis, I'm back in London with no job. I've got some money stashed that I was saving. It wasn't a lot. I'm in a pub with a couple of pounds. What'm I gonna do now? Damn it. It was around 8:30 in the evening.

The company that was promoting Procol Harum in Germany, The Berenbröcks, were really good people. Anna Berenbröck was a really nice black girl—she was lovely. Gorgeous. Looked like a model. She'd walk down the *Strasse* and you'd have to think, "What a stunner." She spoke perfect English. She'd given me her home phone number in Munich.

I just called her on the off chance…"Yo! What's happening?" I said. "Bryan Rooney. I'm stuck in London, haven't got a job. Do you have anything going on?"

She goes, "Oh! Bryan!" This is the truth. "Oh! Hang on. Let me call you back. What's the number?" I had no choice but to give her the public phone number in the pub. I really thought I'd never hear from her.

Five minutes later the pub's public phone rings. I pick it up. It's Anna Berenbröck. "Can you get yourself to Heathrow Airport?"

I said, "Yeah…, I can manage the bus fare."

She said, "Okay. We've got an 11:30 flight for you to Munich, and we'll have a car pick you up." They wanted me because in those days it was a status thing to have an English roadie on their production staff.

I was very lucky, if you think about it. Sometimes you'd come across Germans who weren't too happy with the English because of World War

II. I'd be doing a gig at The Stadthalle in Dingbat-Nowhere, and I'd be next door at The Rathouse having a coupla beers and a bowl of gulasch, and some German would come up and go, "Englander!"

"Yep."

"YOU BOMBED MY HOUSE!"

"It had nothing to do with me, pal." Although my Dad might have! He was in the RAF, God bless 'im. But anyway, Germany started it—it wasn't me. I wasn't shy or scared, "Bug off." I'd get ready to hit him with a mike stand.

So anyway that night I got myself to the airport, and there was a first class ticket waiting! Nice. Yo! I'm off, over to Munich. It's only a 2-hour flight, no big deal. Anna's sittin' outside the airport with a limousine.

This is looking up. She takes me to her beautiful big house. Well…, okay! She's got some food ready for me, gives me some drinks.

"This is your bedroom in here, and tomorrow we'll get all the details. But we've got a job for ya, it'll be nice." So I slept in a nice comfortable bed again. That's the way life is sometimes. I was now with Berenbröcks Production Company.

The Americans Next Door

My neighbors were these 2 American guys who were dealing pot to the U.S. 7th Army. They weren't Army guys themselves, just Americans making money. Yeah, there were drugs. I did drugs. I don't mind sayin' it 'cause it's true. What's the FBI gonna do about it now?

One day the 3 of us drove off in their Mercedes. "Where're we going?"

"You'll see." Bump, bump. We end up in the middle of this forest, parked down in a depression, like a little gully. We're just sittin' there. I said, "What're we waiting for?"

"You'll see."

Then all of the sudden there's all this noise, like we're being invaded. There's rounds whizzing by, tanks, helicopters, the whole gamut. We're in the middle of an Army training exercise! I ducked down a bit but the 2

Americans just sat there like nothing's up. Then an American Army helicopter lands about 20 or 30 feet away from us! Oh no, they've spotted us! The rotors don't stop, and the Army guys hop out and are bent down low, running right toward us. The 2 Americans jump out with this big duffle bag, exchange a few words and stuff with the Army guys, come back to the Mercedes, and the helicopter takes off. They turn back at me in the back seat with big old smiles. "Wasn't that fun?" They had me with that one.

Afterwards I was in hysterics. We all went down to The Piper Club, a private club in Munich that The Berenbröcks and these American guys belonged to. We were all members. It was like Tramps in London. It was great. I was drinking Scotch in those days, and you couldn't just go to the bar and say, "Scotch and Coke." You had to buy liquor by the bottle, and they put your name on it. Then when it's out, you have to buy another bottle. And they'd charge you a *huge* amount of money for it.

Learning German with Bob Nixon

The Berenbröcks sent me to the Berlitz language school in Munich to learn German. It was quite a joke for me. I'd have a joint as they'd drive me to my 9 a.m. class, and there I sat with 2 Koreans, 3 Japanese, a Czechoslovakian, Richard Nixon's nephew Bob Nixon, and Bob's secureity guy.

The way Berlitz works is that you all sit around a long table and you can only speak in the language you're learning—in my case, German. You're not allowed to speak in your own language. The teacher gives you a sentence, and everyone repeats it. The 2 Koreans just had the hardest time. German's a hard, guttural language. It's easier for English people because it's not too different. The Koreans and Japanese just couldn't wrap their vocal cords around it. I couldn't stop laughing. I didn't learn a thing. Well, I did learn, *"Die Aschenbacher liegt auf dem Tisch."* The ashtray lies on the table. Well done, Bryan. And off I went. It was like someone said, "There's Germany. Go. See ya. Here's a map."

"Okay, thanks."

On Tour with Reinhard Mey

The first act The Berenbröcks gave me to tour Germany with was Reinhard Mey. Nobody's heard of him in the U.S. He's the only German person I know who can sing. He's like a Bob Dylan, a storyteller. And the German language is so heavy. "*Ich-bin-ein-Schweinenhund*!" But this guy could sing. He's really a renaissance man. This was 1971, and we were touring for his album *Ich Bin Aus Holz Gemacht*, something like *I'm Made Out of Wood*.

His stage setup was 2 little speakers, 1 guitar, and 2 microphones (1 on his guitar, 1 for himself). That was the whole show. The "sound system" was a little amplifier: on/off, treble, bass. I put the speakers on a bit of a tilt to face the audience. Oh, and 1 mini-spotlight I had to schlep up to the balcony. His songs were all very happy—butterflies and stuff. I was amazed. So I said, "Yeah, okay, I can deal with him."

They gave me a Mercedes as the tour "truck." He played in opera halls and other places that were acoustically beautiful. Even with the little sound system we could fill the places with sound. The audiences were in suits and ties—a sophisticated crowd. It was a cultural thing to go see his concert. I had to stay clean myself: I wore trousers! I even carried a tie with me for afterwards!

Reinhard's wife, a French girl, Christine, was wonderful. They both spoke fluent English, German, and French. She traveled with him in a Porsche. So I've got a Mercedes with the equipment, they're in a Porsche, and that's the crew. That's the gig. This is totally different than what I'm used to.

We're all over Germany. And Reinhard Mey is a gourmet, so the record company, Deiss, would set it up so that wherever we went we got the absolute best restaurant in town after the show, didn't matter what it was. The restaurant would close down and cook incredible meals just for us, and serve the best wine, whatever we wanted. Just him, his wife, me, and the record company people. I've been in some incredible restaurants there, like an abbey that'd been turned into a restaurant. Reinhard was so cool. I always had my nice seat at the restaurant, and he'd buy anything I wanted, it didn't matter. He treated me like an equal. He'd tell stories. He's a beautiful guy.

The shows were 3,000- to 5,000-seaters, and he sold out everywhere. I said, "Sell records in the lobby." Yeah, I'm the one who suggested it. So he did, and he'd sell a million records and stuff in the lobbies. We got some wallies from the record company—junior staff, the kids—to help sell. Merchandising was just coming into vogue. Nobody knew, nobody'd even thought about it. In England they'd just started to do it, and I suggested it to him: "Get a coupla guys from the record company, throw 'em in the car with boxes of records, throw 'em in the lobby with a table as people are leaving or coming in, they'll just buy."

He said, "Brilliant!"

Christmastime Alone in Düsseldorf

I had a great time touring with Rienhard and company. Not quite a year later, still in 1971, we're up in Düsseldorf. It's coming up to Christmas, and it's snowing. The tour's over. Reinhard and his wife go back to France. I've got the Mercedes, I've got a suitcase, and I'm in a hotel.

I'm homesick. I've never been homesick in my life! It's true. I've been all around the world…and I'm in Düsseldorf and I get homesick. Must've been Christmas. So I'm looking at the bottle of schnapps. Should I drink all of that? Or go down to the bar and be civilized and have a beer? Or get into a fight.

I'm just about to go out the door and be civilized, and the phone rings. Oh, well, you never know…so I pick up the phone.

It's Kenny Smith from London, me old Liverpool mate, who got St. James Infirmary to move to London. I hadn't spoken to him in 4 or 5 years. I'd bumped into him in London occasionally. He was doing stuff with The Cream and Clapton and all that, then he got in with Apple. He realized I was working for The Berenbröcks, so he'd phoned them in Munich and got my itinerary, and figured out I was in Düsseldorf.

So he called me. "'Ow are ya? What're you doing?"

"Hanging out in Düsseldorf." You know, Düsseldorf is a nice town …for all the Düsseldorf people. It's nice on a spring day, but in December, well, right then it was cold, kind of dreary, gray, sleeting. It's industrial, Detroitish.

I was used to being away when I was on the road, and when I was working in the Merchant Navy. I was used to being anywhere that I had to be. Maybe it was just Kenny's voice, with the Liverpool accent, "All right boyz! 'Ow are ya?" I was missing the camaraderie, the times sitting in the pub by the fireplace. And I was just missing the language.

Kenny says, "We're coming up to Christmas…."

I say, "Ah, don't start."

And he said, "Right. Don't worry. Do you wanna come home?"

I said, "Why, what's happenin'?"

He said, "I've got a job for you at Apple, with The Beatles."

"Really!"

"Yeah, I'll send you an airline ticket tomorrow."

Well, everyone knows Apple and The Beatles. That's like the top of the pyramid, sod The Stones! But I'm from Liverpool, so I wasn't overly excited about The Beatles in particular. I knew who they were, what they were doing. I'd seen them in Liverpool playing in The Cavern, but I'd never actually go and shake their hands and say, "I think you're great, man!" Because they'd just look at you and brush your arm off their sleeve and go, "What the…? Who is he?"

At this point, end of 1971, The Beatles were still in the process of breaking up. You can't just break up something like The Beatles overnight. Kenny was Ringo's personal assistant. In addition to the band's management staff, all The Beatles had their own personal managers and personal assistants. The job for me was at Apple Corp. directly, the business side of The Beatles.

The Berenbröcks job was a good gig, but fortunately we'd finished that tour, so I wasn't letting anybody down. They'd talked about possibly putting me out on the road that coming spring with Marcel Marceau. I was going to do the sound for a bloody mime! HAHA! Well, he's a mime, but he has music, and cues, and a click track. I was a bit drunk, but I could still think it through: I could run sound for a mime, or…. I'm better off with The Beatles.

I was supposed to go back to Munich in the Merc after the tour, which would've been a helluva drive in winter weather. That's like going from the Oregon border to L.A. I called The Berenbröcks office and said, "The keys to the Mercedes will be at the Düsseldorf Holiday Inn, pick it up at your convenience." I don't think they were really surprised. Anna was a lovely woman, and I think she knew something was coming. I said I was going back to England. She understood—when I mentioned the magic word, Apple.

Working for The Beatles at Apple

Now before I go into what I did at Apple, here's what I know about The Beatles' breakup, what I picked up when I worked there at the tail end of it and afterwards. People try to put an exact date on it, 1970-something, but really they just drifted apart.

Apple Corps formed in September, 1967. In about 1969, The Beatles were embarking on what would become their final record, *Let It Be*. The first Apple building, which had Apple Studios right in the basement, was at 3 Savile Row in the West End. Bond Street was the connecting street at a T junction, that's where the pub was. It's a very, very posh area. Savile Row is famous for handmade clothing. It was the street where all the tailors and custom clothes shops are—500 bucks for a shirt. It's famous worldwide. If you've got money and you want a pair of shoes made, or a shirt, you go to Savile Row. The Beatles filmed videos from the *Let it Be* album on top of the roof, January 30, 1969. I wasn't there. They played a coupla songs before the cops kicked them off. I mean, that neighborhood was posh, guys in bowler hats and all. It was their final live performance as The Beatles.

During the album's recording there's a lot of turmoil. The influx of lawyers was a sign that things were souring, along with different outside accountants coming in to analyze who owned what, where, why.

The next thing you know, this New York guy, Allen Klein, got involved. Initially, I think his job was to straighten out the paperwork. It was tangled. Nobody really knew who owned what. And if they were gonna separate, then everybody should at least know what they owned.

England had a Socialist government then. Harold Wilson was the premier, the prime minister, the bastard. The tax rate for guys who were earning the amount of money that The Beatles earned at one point reached 101%! You can verify it. That means for every dollar they earned, they were paying it all—and another penny on it—to the government. They had *negative* income.

Of course they're all upset, "This is STUPID! This is just looney! We're losin' income!" So they had all these accountants, offshore banking, residences in other countries, and other things. There's lots of places you can put your money before the government gets their hands on it. It's not cheating, it's what you do. Otherwise you'd be in debt to the government because you earned a good living.

As The Beatles' breakup was more final, Apple moved to St. James Street, which was only about 3 blocks away. It was still in an extremely expensive part of London, with all the private gentlemen's clubs, MPs (Members of Parliament), where you have to be a duke or a duchess just to walk through the door. *Serious* limos, the old British Rolls Royces. I'm not talkin' about The Speakeasy or a rock 'n' roll club, we're talkin' about gentlemen's smokin' clubs, cigars…the "Oh, I say, I'll have the beef and a bottle of champagne for breakfast" kinda clubs. And we were right in the middle of it. It was a beautiful regency building, 4 stories plus a basement, with an elevator, which was unusual in those days. In New York you'd call it a brownstone. They owned the whole building, not just a little piece of it, the whole thing.

This was the building that had the Apple accountants, PR, transport, communications, lunacy…. Apple Films was in the basement, by the kitchen. They had a million bucks worth of equipment.

At Apple there'd be meetings with The Beatles and all the lawyers and accountants, which was a constant nuisance. Every day there was another accountant, and they also had outside accountants auditing the books. Arthur Young, big independent accountants, had to come in and audit everything we did, all the cash receipts, everything, because all your expenditures had to be accounted for to the tax people.

I thought the attorneys escalated it to a point where they were running the show. It was like divorce court with 4 people. "The cat's mine!" "No it's not, it's my cat!" Or "I want the dinner service, and you can have...." It's ugly. It wasn't that The Beatles were being ugly to each other, they weren't. It was ugly because of the lawyers. "Well, I represent X and *we* want...." and then you've got somebody else, "No, no, no! *We*, I represent Y...." And then you've got the guy from New York, Allen Klein, going "Well, no, that's all wrong, and this is right," and all that.

It just went on and on until the end. Eventually there was no point in staying together as a unit because they couldn't create together.

Besides, they'd done their fair share. They'd entertained the bloody planet for a long, long time! That's a lot of responsibility. They entertained a *billion* people. They were more than allowed to go off in different directions.

People put a lot of responsibility on them; people just wanted so much from these guys, you know? To the point they were like a religion, God! They couldn't even walk down the street without being buggered and harassed. They loved each other, forever. Always did. And they still worked on each other's projects, helped each other out. Then eventually it became, "You go there, I'll go there," and "Call ya in 6 months." So what? It's their privilege.

They had every right to go in different directions. And I don't care what the *Daily Mail* or the *Mirror* in London said—"They're Leaving Us!" I mean, hang on, they're not going to Mars. They're just carrying on. Give 'em a break already!

I know what you're wondering, and no, I would not say that Yoko Ono caused this. To me, that was always just a rumor. The newspapers and the rags in London would scream, "Yoko Splits The Beatles!" A lot of us just thought, "Well, the rags have got to put the blame on somebody." And Yoko, being an avant-garde Japanese artist with big sunglasses and weird stuff in galleries, made the rags easily say, "She's robbin' John of his money and opening all these galleries up." The rags

49

are useless. She was an easy target. Poor Yoko was takin' the goddamn heat. She was in tears, but it would get to anyone. And she took the heat for a long, long time.

Then it was Linda McCartney's time. "Linda did it! Linda Broke Up The Beatles!"

Well, they could have just as truthfully said I did it! "Bryan Rooney Breaks Up The Beatles! Refuses to Drive Ringo to the Club!" or something like that. Or blame it on someone's dog. It's just stupid.

Personally, I know they'd been together since they were kids, every day living out of each other's pockets. And on top of that, everywhere they went, they couldn't move 'cause of security factors. Especially when they were on the road. That's got to drive you crazy. I mean, I've been on the road as a roadie, but goin' out there as a 4-man band, locked in a cage, day after day after day.... That's what did it. That's understandable: They needed space.

As I said, they still loved each other, and they still really cared about each other, from day 1 'til the very last day. Look at the concert for George after he died. There were tears everywhere. That doesn't just happen for somebody you hate. It's true respect, and love. No, no, anyone who says Yoko was to blame got it wrong.

Back in London: Hired by Apple Corp.

So just before Christmas 1971 I got a plane from Dusseldorf to London. Kenny picked me up in a Rolls Royce and took me to his house. He had a really nice house. We hung out, had some nice food, talked about what'd happened, who was doing what, what was he doing, and why.

And what was the job? He said, "Well, The Beatles need somebody to shuttle them around London."

So he takes me down to Apple for an interview with a guy called Vincent Murphy who was in charge of all the transport. Apple had several top-of-the-line vehicles, no junk cars in there. Apple had their own record company, their own studio. They could do anything they wanted—which they did.

So at the interview the guy says, "Well, do you know London?"

I said, "Yep, I know London."

He says, "Do you *really* know it?"

I said, "Oh, yeah, I *really* know it." Which was a bit of a lie. London's a big place, so only a taxi driver *knows* London.

Vincent said, "Okay! Monday. Start Monday. Um, just come sit in the lobby, and then we'll find you things to do." That was the interview. Kenny'd obviously seriously recommended me. He'd really pumped me up to them. I was to start the 1st Monday of the new year, January 1972.

Vincent says, "Oh, you'll need a car, so take one of the Mini Cooper S's," and gave me the keys. "And you'll need somewhere to live. There's a house not far from Kenny's, he'll show you where it is, there's the keys." It's an Apple townhouse, a Beatles townhouse, in the middle of London: Boston Place #34. It was like a row of mansions with terraced servants' houses at the back. In those days they were *the* places to be, *the* houses to have. The Beatles had houses all over London. Another guy who'd come down from Liverpool with us, Pete Rooney, the drummer from St. James Infirmary, was there too. Kenny had gotten him a job at Apple as well, same kind of thing. We lived in the same house. He was a bit of a conservative bastard, though. Puritan.

Anyway, Vincent says, "So...you need some money?"

I said, "Yeah...."

"Here you go." And he gave me a whole bunch—a whole wad of money! And said, "There you go. We'll see you Monday."

I was so relieved that the job looked *stable*. I wasn't schlepping equipment, driving trucks, and shoutin' and screamin' with Germans. They'd given me a house, and a car, and a bunch of money. I was happy...and I was a bit nervous, 'cause I wasn't too sure what I was gonna be doing.

"Don't worry, we'll find stuff for you to do. Just come back Monday and you'll be fine. Have a nice weekend with Kenny, 'cause I know you've been in Germany. Come back Monday, and we'll sort out what's happening."

51

"Okay."

Monday I drove down to Apple, parked my little Mini Cooper at the curb, vroom, vroom, nice. Lovely. Went in, sat down in the lobby. Okay…? Lunchtime comes, and a whole bunch of people come out of Apple's offices, and they all go to the pubs or somewhere for lunch. So I went out for lunch. Came back from lunch, sat in the lobby. Everybody left. I went home. That was my first day at Apple.

This went on for a full week. I'd just come in every morning at the right time and sit down in the lobby. Nobody said a word to me! The security guy, Charlie "Sergeant" Swain, was about 90 years old, dressed in a uniform like a British Admiral/doorman. He was a *serious* veteran, with World War I medals, a tank driver. He carried all these medals with pride, God bless 'im. He was a bit shaky; liked his gin as well. He couldn't stop a rabbit, but he was security. And he was a right old cranky git. But he let me in 'cause he knew I was workin' there.

At the end of the week one of the secretaries, Joan Woodgate, came over and said, "We don't mind people hangin' out in the lobby…" 'cause outside there were Apple Scruffs. You know George Harrison's song, "Apple Scruffs," is about all the girls who used to sit outside and just wait until somebody'd turn up and say hello. They'd be there all day, every day, on the steps to the office, just to see The Beatles. They were…fondly… known as Apple Scruffs, and George wrote that beautiful song about 'em. Yeah, it was fond, but think about it. Every day of your life—I mean every day—these people are there on your front steps, not doing anything, just sittin' there waiting for a car to pull up with a Beatle in it. There were some guys, but it was mostly girls. You couldn't even get out of your car without going through a gauntlet. Every day. There was no "back door." Ringo, for one, went to the office every day. The Scruffs were mostly Americans. They'd come over and spend their whole vacation sitting on the steps at Apple, three months sometimes. Then they'd go and there'd be other ones taking their place. We'd maybe give 'em albums and stuff. It would rain and snow on them, so we'd give 'em a bowl of soup or something.

So anyway, Joan says, "We don't mind people hangin' out in the lobby, but, you know, you've been coming here every day now for a week. So would you mind moving? You've gotta go. This is crazy."

She thought I was just hangin' out, drinkin' a coffee. I said, "But I WORK here!"

She goes, "No!"

"Yeah, I do! Go up and see Vincent who gave me the job."

"Oh! Well, if you *work* here, hang on!" She scuttled off to her office and came back with a bunch of bookwork and stuff. "Right! C'mon, you can take me to the bank. I've got a bunch of stuff to do."

I said, "Okay, that's cool."

"Where's your car?"

"Right there."

"You shouldn't park there! Anyway, okay, c'mon." So I jumped in the car and took her to one of the banks, where she had to drop off a bunch of books and paperwork.

I brought her back from the bank to Apple and within an hour she'd passed the word around there was a new driver in the lobby. Nobody had their own car in those days. So everyone's comin' down to me. "I need to go to the donut shop." Wherever—I didn't mind. I was gettin' paid.

So that went on for a about a year, me just drivin' people all over goddamn Central London. I never saw Ringo or anybody, though I would've liked to say "Hello! How are ya?" to them.

Apple Corp. built a kitchen and gave jobs in it to 2 of the Apple Scruffs from America. It was a beautiful kitchen, all stainless steel everywhere, and a dining room for all us guys, the secretaries, production, and whoever was in. Anything you wanted you could just order—anything. Apple had accounts with Harrods and all the big posh stores. If Ringo wanted sand dabs, they'd just pick up the phone and Harrods would deliver. If you wanted chateaubriand, you got it. They made their own things in the kitchen too. It was open all day and you'd just wander in and say, "A cheese sandwich with tomatoes, please, and a beer." It didn't matter what you wanted. There was no point in being shy about it, you just asked. If I said I wanted filet mignon, I'd get filet mignon. Apple really took care of their people. And whoever was in town would drop by and eat too—The Who, The Stones. They'd just walk in.

Us guys had some kind of status, 'cause we were next to the boys. We were in charge of doing the boys' stuff. So we were quite high up on the totem pole. We'd run the girls around to the banks and stuff too—whatever it took to keep things moving, to keep everyone happy. It was our job.

Tumbling Down George Harrison's Stairs

The first Beatle I met was George Harrison. Apple's Account Department gave me an envelope and a set of directions to George's house, Friar Park, which was about 60 miles west of London in a place called Henley on Thames. It's a beautiful river town, with rowing boats, swans, beautiful 14th-century bridges. Even the pubs are older than most dynasties.

I was to deliver the cash for the gardeners and the workmen, several thousand pounds. George was redoing the whole house, so there were a lot of workers. In those days people didn't get paid by check, they got paid cash. You'd get a little brown envelope with your name on it and your money tucked in it. You didn't have to deal with a bank. All the people who were working at George's house needed to be paid every Friday.

I get to George's house to a *huge* set of gates. I get through the gates, and take a long winding driveway up to this castle which is covered in scaffolding. There's work and dirt, and there's people everywhere.

I get out the car and say, "I'm lookin' for George."

Someone said, "Oh, you have to use the back, the servant's entrance."

So I get me payroll bag, go around the back, go through the kitchen entrance, and there's a couple of girls cookin' and ironing clothes and stuff. "Lookin' for George."

One girl goes, "Go over there to the East Tower, gonna be a big oak door, just go through the door, up the steps. At the top of the steps there's another oak door. Knock on the door, George'll be there because that's where he's living while they're doing all this renovation. He has an apartment up there." Everything was torn apart. The castle's got about 20 bedrooms and a hallway you could dance in. It's *very large*. It's not a house, it's a mansion, castle. It's beautiful.

So I go "Okay, no problem. Thank you." The girl thought he was expecting me. Toddle along, go down the hall, up the stairs, knock on the door. I hear water running and all that, maybe Pattie was making tea.

The door opens. George Harrison's standing there, and he goes, "Who the fuck are you?"

"Pardon?"

Boom. He hits me! And I roll down the tower, which is all flagstone from something like the 17th century, still clutching the bag of money, 'cause that's vital—I never let go of money! I hit the door at the bottom. I'm bruised to say the least.

He's at the top of the stairs goin', "YOU FUCKIN' IDIOT! Coming to my door!"

Well, I said, "That's crazy! See you!"

So I open the other door at the bottom and go out and there's this guy in jeans, with an afro. And he goes, "What's going—what's all the howlin'—what's the noise?"

I said, "Who are you?"

He said, "I'm Terry Doran, George's personal manager."

"Great! Give him that! And tell him to stick it while he's at it!"

"What happened?"

"I went up there, I've got the payroll for all your goddamn gardeners and workers and glaziers and whoever you've got. I've got thousands of pounds. And he punches me! He just punched me down the stairs!"

He said, "No! Nobody's supposed to go up there."

"Well, the girls in the kitchen sent me up there to deliver the wages."

He said, "They're not supposed to! I get—I'm in charge! Come to my office." He's got his own little office where the whole operation's running from. "I'm so embarrassed." He puts the money in a safe, and he goes, "Right! I'm so embarrassed! C'mon, out, let's go."

"Where're we goin'?"

"Pub." It's England, you know: Problem? Not a problem, we'll sort it out in the pub.

So we get in his BMW and he screams down the driveway like a Formula 1 driver. Ducks and chickens and stuff are goin' everywhere. We go through the gates, down the hill, to the river. There's a beautiful pub called The Angel right on the Angel Bridge on the River Thames.

He says, "Let's go in here, we'll have lunch, you'll be all right." He's from Liverpool as well! We have a few drinks, and the food is fabulous. It's a very expensive pub, it's not like your local darts-and-mud. This one was exceptional, with carpets…a *serious* pub. You had to know the owner to get in.

He said, "What're we gonna do?"

I said, "I don't know. I've got to get back to Apple."

"You can't go back all injured like that!"

"What d'you mean?"

"No, no, I can't have that." So he picks up the phone on the bar and phones Apple. He speaks to Gerald, who's in charge of petty cash. "Jerry! Right! I've got Bryan Rooney here. He's stayin' overnight. You don't need him? So he's with us for the time being. Yeah, you know, had a little problem, but I'll take care of him."

"Oh, okay, that's all right," Jerry says. You know, it's whatever The Beatles want. If George wants Bryan, George gets Bryan. It's no big deal.

Terry says to me, "How's that, then? You're stayin' here!"

I says, "The place is a wreck!"

"Oh no, no! We've got some nice rooms."

We go back, and by this time George is actually dressed, with gorgeous Pattie Harrison, sittin' downstairs in the kitchen.

Terry goes, "What're you doin? You can't go around kickin' people down stairs! It's bad for business!"

They go, "What?"

"*He* works for *us*. He's *our* guy."

"Well he's—but—!"

I said, "Look, nobody told me not to go up to your apartment. In fact, I was sent there. I wouldn't have gone near you if I'd have known I was gonna get kicked down a flight of bloody flagstone steps from the 17th century."

George stood up and said, "I'm really sorry, man. Obviously it won't happen again," and all that. He knew I was annoyed, and it's not in him to be violent. He'd only just woken up, and Pattie was still in her nightgown, and he didn't wanna know nothin'. And with all the noise and the construction and stuff going on, the last thing he needed was a stranger knockin' on his apartment door. Ordinarily nobody would even get *that* far, except I had the payroll bag and I was from Apple, and they knew it was wage day and I was perfectly legitimate.

I says, "Well, that's all right. That's cool. It's cool."

"Tell you what," George says. "We'll all go out for dinner tonight. Where're you gonna put him, Terry?"

"The Priest's Room."

"Okay, that's a good one." In the Revolution, when Cromwell was taking over England, they were slaughtering priests—Catholics, Protestants. They didn't want any priests in the country. So in the mansions and castles the priests always had their own room with a bolt hole in it, like a secret door, where they could go and hide.

Terry takes me along and says, "There, you can have that room." The room is made up immaculately, a fabulous room with a 4-poster bed. "This is your room while you're here. And later on we'll go for dinner."

Then Terry took me around the gardens, and introduced me to 2 Dobermans, Adolf and Göring. He says, "You'd better get to know them, 'cause they'll rip your throat out."

"Oh…. Nice doggies." I gave 'em a biscuit so they got to know me.

Some of the gardens were starting to come together. Friar Park was a real weird, brilliant place, that had been left to wrack and ruin. Sir Frank Crisp, the guy who built it, was a total lunatic. George refurbished it with the original plans. There was a lake, and tunnels that went underneath islands on the lake. In the tunnel, when you looked up, you'd see this glass-bottomed fish pond. It was like Disney. You could punt through the tunnel on little boats, row through an island, and above you were fish. There was a scale model of The Eiger, the mountain in Switzerland, behind the house. There was a main lake with islands and ponds around with koi fish and the sun shining through. And there were waterfalls forever. Incredible! Not many people have seen this place. George never let anyone see it.

I ended up staying at Friar Park about 4 days. That was my introduction to George.

George would always say, "Om," from his Indian influences. It means a lot, actually. Ommmmm. He said it if something nice happened, or something went his way, or you did something nice for him. Maybe you just fed the dogs correctly: "Ommmmmmm." And he'd smile, and you'd smile back, and the sky was blue, the grass was green…it was all beautiful.

Tending Bar for Ringo Starr

When I met Ringo, he was having a *big* party at his house in North London. His street had big houses; not estates, just big houses. I was corralled into being the barman.

Lulu was there, Eric Clapton, Cilla Black, George, DeeDee the BBC music show hostess. They were all there. Well, except Paul was off somewhere, and Yoko didn't socialize that much in terms of, "Let's just have a party, play some music as loud as we can, and have a good time." I think she was a lot more reserved than that.

I had to be up there in the afternoon to load all the drinks and set up the bar. Kenny, Ringo's assistant and my good buddy, God bless him, introduces me.

Ringo says, "Okay! Carry on! Set up over there. Whatever you're doing just do it, and thank you."

So off I went, set up the bar—at least I knew how to do that as well, apart from my other talents! Then everybody starts arriving. Lulu lived like 2 doors away on the same street. She did really well. She was a lovely Scottish girl, like a female Rod Stewart, with a beautiful voice. Her big songs were, "To Sir With Love" and "Shout!" She did quite a few good movies. She didn't care about anything. "Hallo, what's happenin'?" She'd just push you out the way if you were between point A and B.

People like that showed up at this party. For every drink I'm giving them, I'm taking one, but it's no problem and nobody cares because it's all one big zoo.

Ringo stopped by the bar and said, "Nice to see you. How are you?" And then later, "You work for us?"

I said, "Yeah. I'm down at the office and all that. I've got the little Mini Cooper."

He says, "Oh, you can take any car you want! It doesn't matter. Whatever you feel comfortable with."

He's really generous, Ringo, to the nth degree. He always went out of his way to introduce himself and make people comfortable. At the party there were a lot of wives and girlfriends who had never been to his house before, and he'd go and say hello and stand with them. He was the perfect host.

Ringo was so genial, so friendly, generous to a fault. I sound like a record stuck on one track, but he was caring. He cared about how *you* were. He'd say, "How's your family?" Or, "I know you've got sisters, are they okay? Do they need some 8-tracks I can send up to them?"

I'd say, "Oh, no, it's okay, they're fine."

Literally on a daily basis he'd cheer people up. He had his own beautiful office in Apple, 'cause by that time he was the only guy who went there on a regular basis, pretty much every day. He'd wander around with his tea, very jovial, say hello to everybody. You just feel comfortable around the guy. Always.

Driving John Lennon's Psychedelic Rolls

A week later I'm down at the office and the world-famous psychedelic Rolls Royce pulls up outside of Apple. I'm just sitting in the lobby hanging out with my cigarette—in those days, you could smoke in buildings in England. Thank God!

I go leaping out 'cause part of my job was to park the cars. Outside of Apple there was a red line, no parking, so you had to go and move 'em, either to a parking meter if it was a short visit, or take the vehicle over to a garage we rented where we stored and rented spaces for all the vehicles.

We had about 34 vehicles, serious cars. There were 4 Mini Cooper S's, a Mercedes 600 Pullman, Mercedes 190SL Sports and 280SL Coupe, Bentley Continentals. You name it, we had it. A lot of times I'd have to choose which one based on what the job was, what the gig was, where we were going. If it's a formal thing, we'd need this vehicle, if it's just casual, going down to pub for a game of darts, then we'd take that vehicle.

So of course John Lennon gets out the psychedelic Rolls and I go, "Yo! Hello. Give me the keys, I'll garage it."

He goes, "Well, who are you?"

I says, "New guy, Bryan Rooney."

"Oh! Pleasure! Nice to see ya…. Ya okay with that car?" 'Cause he really liked it.

"Oh, yeah, I've got a license, I'm cool."

"Okay. Nice. Thanks a lot." And he went inside.

John was living out in Ascot, Royal Ascot at Tittenhurst Park, an hour and a half from Apple, mainly because of the traffic. London is a busy, busy town. So once you get into the suburbs or into town it's very crowded—unless you really know the routes, like we did, the drivers. We knew all the little back alleys, where you wouldn't normally take a psychedelic Rolls Royce, 'cause you'd be worrying about clipping it. But we knew to an inch. We were good drivers!

He really did like that Rolls. It was beautiful. John's Mercedes 600 Pullman was the one that he'd fitted a Tannoy system underneath the hood—metal Tannoy horns, and a microphone and an amplifier. So if he was stopped at lights or something he'd go, "'Ello! 'Ow are ya?" And people would spin around 'cause it'd be blaring out the front of the vehicle. This was his idea of a great time, shouting at people: "Get away!" or "Oy, you stupid-looking git!" You know, John Lennon could do and say whatever he wanted. He was very sarcastic, a right hooligan. Anyway,

John had the Pullman and all sorts of vehicles, but he liked to pose around London in this huge psychedelic Rolls.

Rolls Royce Motor Cars Ltd. were not amused, 'cause of course the car was splashed everywhere, in every newspaper: John and Yoko with their sunglasses on here, showing it to pedestrians there. It was quite a scene. Rolls Royce were quite upset with the "upgrades," and sent him letters like, "You can't do that to one of our cars. It's not part of the warranty."

His response was, "So what? I don't care! What're you gonna do, take it away from me? I bought it. It's my car."

"Well, you've broke the warranty and...."

And he'd say, "Oh, I can always find a Rolls Royce mechanic, retired, or whatever. So don't bug me." He framed the letters.

John Lennon was a strong guy, but wasn't domineering. He was gentle, intelligent. I mean, this guy went to a university, in Liverpool. And for what you might say about Liverpool, they have great universities. He was very well-read. And he had a lot of social agendas.

John was just in trouble everywhere, and I'm a troublemaker, born and bred, so I got along with John real well on that level.

John used to say, "You silly git!" Like if you'd make a wrong turn. "Git" is like, "you fool!" in England. It wouldn't be said sternly, like "You are an idiot," but kindly: "You silly git. What're we doing on this street? We should be on that street. What are you, daft, or something?"

And you'd go, "Oh, no, I'm sorry man," 'cause you're driving John Lennon! You don't want to make a mistake. You just want to get on with it, deliver him to the doorstep as close as can. To open the door and, as smoothly as you can, get him inside without any hassle. You wanted everyone to get on and make it easier for him, or whoever I was doing it for. A part of the credo was to make it easy for these guys, 'cause they had enough on their plates without worrying about how to get somewhere, where to park, what table are they going to be at. They didn't *need* to worry about all that stuff.

John Lennon really wanted to "give peace a chance." As for all those beautiful songs he had, he really meant them. He wasn't just like, "This'll be a number 1." He was committed to peace; he really did believe. And he knew the power he had, and thought he had to use his power to try and change things. It was very heavy. To me, he always was above the kings and presidents. If anyone—world-famous musicians—was going to be in front of the antiwar effort it had to be The Beatles, and if anyone from The Beatles had to be in front it was Lennon. He was tailor-made.

Meeting Paul McCartney

I met Paul McCartney at the Apple office too. I didn't park his car, he just turned up. He walked in and did the usual wander around; they'd all wander around their empire. There was the Telex room, so they'd always pop in, go "Hi, how's the Telex room?"

"Oh, fine thank you."

We drivers had our own little office. We were in charge of whatever they wanted, like mega-gophers. He opened the door and said, "Oh, hello, what's going on in here?"

I go, "I'm the new driver."

"Oh! Nice to see you. Welcome."

Overall, Paul and I really didn't click. You know, you can't be best friends with everybody. But he was the type that if somebody in the street came up to him and asked him for an autograph, he'd go, "Oh, yeah! Here ya go!" No problem, you know, he was a Liverpool lad. Still is.

Paul and Linda had a big house—everything's *big*—in Regent's Park very close to Abbey Road Studios. It was a beautiful mansion, no huge grounds or anything, just a nice little garden for the dog to run in. And that was his in-town house. His guy, Hamish, his personal manager, lived there as well. Paul also bought a farm in Scotland. He used to travel to the farm, but if he was doing business in town—in London—then he had a beautiful house there to stay in.

All The Beatles had their own individual projects as well, and had their own individual studios. Paul's studio was up at his farm, where he recorded the *Ram* record, his first solo release after The Beatles. He was the first to release a post-Beatles solo record.

They all had—and Paul and Ringo still have—their own charities. Not many people hear about them, like Save the Children, but I know that Ringo, and I think Paul as well, are literally financing several villages, not just one kid with a photograph. They have trust funds set up to save whole villages. They're in that league.

I knew George Martin, but he was with the studio in the other building, at Savile Row, before we moved to St. James. He didn't actually work for Apple, he worked independent. Even after EMI and Capitol, everybody wanted George Martin. He's a great producer. So he was earning a very nice living, thank you, just being George Martin. He worked with Badfinger, and others…so many bands. A record company would go, "Right…can you produce these?" And he would say, "Yes, sign here. Thank you." He was a gentleman.

So eventually I met all The Beatles. The Beatles were 4 guys, each one with a particular talent. You've got a lot of complex relationships. But everybody at Apple was part of Apple. They had a great environment, not just because of who you're working for, but because when you walked in, it was a family.

Helping Ringo's Assistant Kenny Smith

In addition to The Beatles management, Allen Klein at this point, each Beatle had a manager and also their own personal assistant—to manage their personal lives and keep them happy. John had a great American guy from New York, Alan, who was very, very clever and very into it. Paul had Hamish, a Scottish guy.

Ringo's personal manager was Hilary Gerrard, and he dealt with the money, the contracts, why didn't he get this percentage from that album, the business stuff. That was a tough gig. It was like having lawyers hanging off your sleeves all day.

Me old mate Kenny Smith was Ringo's personal assistant, and I gradually became Kenny's assistant. Kenny was so busy, he needed somebody else to help him. The personal assistants were in charge of all the scheduling for their guy, to run their personal life, keep the diary. In charge of things like, "You have to be at the hairdresser's," and then they could transfer that job to their assistant, or to one of us drivers, to go get the hairdresser or whatever person the appointment was with and take 'em to the Beatle. Basically, you'd go to the hairdresser's, pick him or her up, and bring the hairdresser to the office or to their house. Because it's kind of unseemly to be sitting in a barber shop getting your hair cut when you're a billionaire. I'd pick 'em up and say, "Come on." They were more than happy to just jump in the back of a Rolls Royce.

So in addition to taking care of everybody like I used to do, I also started to help Kenny. I'd go wherever people wanted help, do whatever they needed. It didn't matter what I was doing, I was paid by Apple. I was lucky because what they wanted me to help with got more and more interesting. But I was really a legger, what you now call a gopher!

And I also did a lot of stuff for Terry Doran, George's personal manager, at Friar Park. He was the one who helped me out when George knocked me down the stairs. Terry's an ex-car salesman, but a very, very elegant guy. Nice suits, always.

Terry and Pattie were so busy putting Friar Park together and furnishing it, I spent a *lot* of time with Terry and Pattie just helping them move things. Or the 3 of us would take the Rolls and go all over England getting antique furniture at old pubs. Pattie knew antiques, and there were a lot of beautiful pieces at pubs that were getting demolished or remodeled—grand old bars with big mirrors in them, that sort of thing. We'd find notice of them and go save the furniture from the wrecking ball.

Elvis for President

Once while I was working for Ringo and we were in Los Angeles for something, Elvis came to L.A. too. Ringo and I bumped into him in a hotel; it might have been The Beverly Wilshire. It was me and Ringo just hanging out, then there were hosts of security people. "What's all this?" And then Elvis appeared.

He invited us to Graceland, so we went. But it was so phony. Now, this was before he grassed up John Lennon to the government for smoking pot. God bless Elvis, he's dead now. But he's going, "They're a bunch of drug addict peaceniks" while he's popping every pill known to mankind. And he's grassing people up, saying, "John Lennon smoked pot in my presence," which could've gotten John deported.

If Elvis had survived all his drugs and pills and Tennessee whiskey, and lost some pounds...God, he might be a senator now! President! HAHA! Imagine that!

Harry Nilsson: The *Real* Fifth Beatle

Harry Nilsson was actually in banking in America, initially, a clerk behind the counter. He did some demos, and I think RCA produced an album with him. He made beautiful music. The man had so much talent, and a really weird way of doing things. He was incredibly logical. He knew a lot of stuff. He could tell you Beethoven's birthday…all sorts of weird stuff you wouldn't even think about. He really knew dates. You could give him a date, say, June the 1st, 1641, and he would tell you, "On that date…," and that it was a Monday or whatever. Any date. He was good at card tricks too. He's really an incredible guy.

Ringo was over in America and heard the album, and thought, "This guy has got a great voice, and great songs, and writes." And Ringo is used to writers 'cause he's got the other 2…the other 3! Maybe even 4 if you include George Martin.

So Ringo knew writing, even though he didn't write a lot himself. The Beatles loved Harry, so Ringo flew him over to England. I picked him up and was put in charge of him, which means, "Make sure he doesn't die," and "deliver him where we want him, when we want him, there's the schedule." For me it was no problem, just an extra body to move around. He had enough to do in London that he bought a flat there. He'd lend it out to other musicians sometimes.

Harry was thrilled to be at Apple Records, with The Beatles. But he wasn't intimidated. I think once he got to England and he got in the studio and started pumping out his stuff, everybody just went, "Whoa, what's that?" Harry was a true, true, talent.

Harry was a gorgeous man. Taught me a lot. He'd say, "You stupid git!" He picked up a lot of English stuff. But what else would you do when you're hanging around with a bunch of guys from Liverpool, you know? It kinda gets into ya. Harry was always like, "Guys, all right! We can do it!" Like when we were making the *Son of Dracula* movie and we had to be at the studio at 6:30 in the morning, he'd say, "Aw, come on! We can do it. No problem! We can get there. We can make it." And he always did make it.

I wanted to talk to Ringo about putting another Beatles concert tour together around 1972, with Harry Nilsson in The Beatles, put him up front as a lead singer. Which is a great concept…except Harry Nilsson had never been on stage in his life. He was terrified, had a phobia. He never did a public appearance, ever. But I didn't know that! What a nutter. The only time he was ever in public was, as I mentioned earlier, in Ringo's *Son of Dracula*. I'll come back to that movie.

Harry was a good, good friend of Ringo's, but he'd never been on stage, ever. He hadn't even appeared in a high school band. He was a studio dude. Front The Beatles! It was very selfish of me, really. I wanted to get out on the road, meet some women…!

So this is the *real* 5th Beatle that everybody always talked about. Harry Nilsson. It would have been brilliant.

But by then it was almost to the point that you couldn't get the 4 of them, The Beatles, in a room together. I'd see them come and go. Ringo's office was like ground zero when all this was happening.

The Beatles all had beautiful offices, but Ringo's office had the big conference table. And he had the staff, and he was there all the time, so his operation ran really nicely. He was also the intermediary. One would say, "Could you tell Paul I'm not doin' that, but I'll do this." And then Ringo would speak to Paul.

Ringo was put in the middle of this maelstrom of different ideas, different ways it should go for the entity of Apple itself. How do you break up Apple? Who gets the rights? You'd hear things like, "Who paid for the building?" "I didn't." "Did I pay for this building?" "I don't know, I just moved here." And here's John, "Well, I've always gone into this building through the front door, me and my Rolls Royce, do I own it…?" Then it's numbers-crunchin' time. And here I'm wanting to get a tour together with Harry Nilsson…but it just wouldn't work.

Almost Fired by Allen Klein

As far as The Beatles management, after Brian Epstein, Allen Klein took over, when Apple was at St. James Street. He was a big mob-looking guy from New York with 2 gorillas—bodyguards. Well, one time he came to London and was staying at The Inn on the Park, right by Hyde Park, presidential suite or whatever. And none of his guys would drive in London, so Ringo loaned me to him as a driver in one of Apple's Rolls for the week or 2 he was in town.

One night Allen said, "Pick us up at 7, and take us to town, then we'll go to The Hilton on Park Lane for dinner, then to some clubs." Right. So I was there at 7, and he didn't show. I waited an hour. None of the guys, especially Ringo, would ever leave anyone hanging for over an hour like that, they'd call down to the bell guy and say, "Right, we're hung up here, come back in half an hour" or whatever.

I waited till 8 or so, and about 15 minutes past 8 I asked the bell guy to ring him up. "WHAT?!" he says.

"This is Bryan Rooney, you asked me to be here at 7, what's the program, what's happenin'?"

He screams, "NONE OF YOUR FUCKIN' BUSINESS!" and hangs up the phone.

Well, I don't have to put up with that, so I left.

Next day I'm at Apple, sitting in the lobby, smoking a cigarette, and in storms Allen Klein. "YOU!" he shouts, "YOU'RE FIRED!" Then he storms up to Ringo's office.

Oh, okay… I'm fired from Apple. I say to Joan, Ringo's executive secretary, "I'll be in The Blue Post," which was the pub right around the corner from Apple on Berwick Street.

Joan told me later that when Klein stormed in to Ringo's office, Ringo says, "What's all the fuss about, then?"

Klein says, "Your guy, Bryan Looney, whatever his name is, left me hangin' last night, and I fired him."

Ringo says, "WHAT?!" Ringo got angry, which doesn't happen very often at all, but everyone had been unhappy with Klein for a long time. Ringo says, "Bryan's MY guy! You can't fire MY guy! You have no authority to be hiring and firing! Get out!"

And Joan said Ringo threw Klein out. That was the beginning of the end of Klein working for Apple.

Then Ringo asks Joan where I am, and she says, "The pub."

Ringo comes over to the pub. "Hey, man, what happened?"

So I filled him in, and he says, "Right, man, you don't have to be treated like that. You're not fired. C'mon, let's have some lunch, then back to work."

About a week later Ringo brought in Hilary Gerrard and fired Allen Klein. A bootleg of George Harrison's song "Beware of Darkness" includes a line "beware of ABKCO," Klein's company.

Working at Tittenhurst Park

What's left of Apple at that point is a leased building for administration. The recording studio was leased, so that was shut down. And they closed our building, the Apple building on St. James, and the accountants got transferred to another office building. They're still there on a daily basis playing with the numbers, because the money and the numbers still go to Apple, their flagship, which is still The Beatles' company. You have to have some instrument to divide the money, to put in bank accounts here and there. You can't just have random money getting mailed to somebody and it's not theirs, or it is theirs and they want more. You have to have a structure.

People were let go. If there's no job, there's no job. But I was still with Ringo. Kenny was still his personal assistant, and I was Kenny's assistant. Basically what they wanted—whatever they wanted—was my job to do it, or get it done. Off we went, did it. I still lived in Ringo's Apple house in London, and also stayed at a place at Tittenhurst. It was like I had 4 cars and 2 houses…but none of it was actually mine.

I did all the driving and the running around and the organizing and all. Kenny'd give me a list, and say, "Do this," and I'd go, "Okay, I can deal with that." Ringo had a family, the kids, and his wife, and his house. So he didn't wanna deal with the daily errands and stuff.

John and Yoko had been living at Tittenhurst Park, a huge country estate they'd bought. You've seen it in *The White Album* and some of John's videos, when he's sitting with his piano in a pure white room. The whole house was white, like walking into a cloud. White carpets, white piano, white TV, white walls—everything was white. That was John and Yoko.

John's personal manager Dan Richter lived there too and ran that estate. They had cottages and stables, and a Tudor house down in the grounds which was actually a cricket pavilion. But obviously John had no use for a cricket pitch, and John and Yoko were always into nature, "Peace! Let everything grow," so they just let this whole place get overgrown. It never got mowed, there were no pathways, it just grew forever. As it happened it became beautiful wild English countryside, though with the typical 8-feet-high weeds. It was 82 acres of weeds! They had badgers and foxes and rabbits. It was a wonderful place. And there was a local pub just around the corner called The Nag's Head which did great English lunches, so was very popular with the staff and the crew.

And then Ringo bought John Lennon's estate, Tittenhurst Park, I think sometime in 1972 or 1973. Obviously they were friends. Ringo wanted more room, and John was settling in New York, so Ringo purchased that and we all moved out there.

They had a row of cottages, and barns. Kenny had one of the cottages, and I lived down at the cricket pavilion. Yoko had done it all in white, and when Ringo bought it his wife Maureen immediately started decorating it.

Ringo wanted it to look like parkland, not the bloody English weeds, so you could actually walk around in it. We bought tractors and trailers and all sorts of weird equipment. I'm not a farmer! But we bought it, and off we went, mowing the lawn with gang mowers. Someone says, "Put that 12-man gang mower…." I go, "What is he talkin' about?" So there was something else to do, figure out the hydraulics on the big Ford 5000 with all these implements and farming gear. And off we went! We were digging lily ponds and stuff, maintained the lawns, and got it all back together where you could actually use the 82 acres.

Ringo had been recording with other bands, doing his own stuff. As they say in Liverpool, you've gotta keep your eye in. He's Ringo Starr, you know, what're you gonna do? A lot of people really wanted him on their albums 'cause the guy is like a metronome, a beautiful drummer. And he had his own studio at Tittenhurst, and he'd spend hours a day in there playing around. It was in the house, totally sealed off. John had put it in and then Ringo upgraded it. It was a very nice little studio.

Ringo Buys All of Ludwig's Pigskins

Ringo and John Bonham and Stewart Copeland were all hanging around together. Ludwig made several lines of drumheads, and Ringo always used their pigskins—yes, actual pigskins—for his drums 'cause he felt they gave him a better response, better depth. And he'd used them since he was a kid, 'cause that's all that was available. Now it's all plastics, nylons, webbed. John Bonham used plastics. But Ringo didn't like any of that stuff. Every drummer's different, like every guitarist is different.

Then Ringo heard Ludwig were going to cancel the pigskin drumheads line because they weren't selling enough. The word came down the mill, all through the industry. And Ringo goes, "Aw, what am I gonna do? I hate this plastic…crap."

So we got in touch with Ludwig and bought up the remaining stock of the pigskins. Thousands of them! Well, not thousands…but a *lot* of drumskins. We had them shipped to Tittenhurst Park. I mean, if they were gonna close the line, there wouldn't be any left for anybody else anyway.

But I heard down the grapevine that some other guys were slightly… annoyed…that Ringo had bought everything! They're gonna last him for a good amount of years. And these guys are gonna have to switch because they didn't have the forethought to stock up.

How to Build a Lake in 3 Easy Steps

This is how I remember it. Once we'd mowed the grounds all back from when John was living there, there was a depression in the ground, the part of the cricket pavilion that was the pitch. The pavilion was a beautiful Tudor building, bigger than most people's houses, with showers and kitchen facilities. When people played cricket, they'd all go and sit on the balcony and drink tea and go, "Oh, jolly good!"

Ringo goes to one of the guys, "I don't play cricket. What'm I gonna do with that? Build me a lake." Then he goes off to the Bahamas or somewhere for a while to record with Eric Clapton or something.

The guy says to me, "Well, fine, we need a lake."

And I go, "Oh...okay.... Right."

How do you build a lake? I didn't know! We didn't know. Build a fucking lake! Is there a book, *How to Build a Lake in 3 Easy Steps*? No, there isn't.

So we got quite clever about it. We rented a pitch marker to paint white lines on the grass, then staggered around for a couple of acres with this pitch marker and made white lines. "We're gonna need an inlet, for a boat." Doo doo doo, "That'll do."

"Gotta have an island!" So we went in a bit and did another squiggly circle, "Right, okay, that looks kinda good." It's a couple of acres big.

Then we phoned up the local earthmoving people. "See all the earth between those white lines? Get rid of it." But first we had to build a road. We had to knock down a section of wall, 'cause the whole estate's walled by 8-foot-high, 17th century brick, stone, and stuff. It was a beautiful wall with hedgerows and ivy. We had to knock down a big section, but we saved every brick we knocked down.

They laid a wooden plank road to this space outlined by white lines. They brought in all this heavy equipment and just dug it up, dug it up..., and got rid of it.

We had this huge hole in the ground with an island on it. Good! Right! So then we dig a well. You've gotta fill it, you can't fill acres of lake from the tap, you know. Then you have to get permits. We never thought about all this permits stuff. "This goes here, and you hafta do that, and what're you affectin', how diddly...." Anyway, we managed to bribe and talk our way into a well permit. Then you have to get somebody to sink the well.

Finally we start pumping water. "Hey, this is nice!" Fill it up. It's all murky and muddy, obviously, 'cause it's…muck. So we got it done, go to the pub, have dinner, go to bed.

Come back next morning…the thing is empty. "Uh…oh. Now what?" It's just soaked all the way back into the ground! Right? It's just gone! Millions of gallons, if not millions, a *lot* of water.

God! We don't know what to do! So…go to pub, is the answer. Go to pub. I say, "Calm down, calm down."

Me mate says, "What d'you mean *me* calm down, you're…!"

I said, "Well, it's not gonna do us any good to go looney on this."

What the…heck! So we're sitting in the pub, having a ploughman's lunch. And there's a little TV in the pub, which was highly unusual for an English pub. Still is. There's a commercial on for this big petrochemical company in Europe. It's a huge company…whom I'll leave unnamed. And they were helping out in Bangladesh, where there'd been a drought and famine. They were showing a corporate commercial about how cool they were to mankind…even though they're making the worst chemicals known to mankind. They're doing this big PR thing with this rubber liner thing, and they're lining acres of land in Bangladesh 'cause when it does rain, it's gonna hold the water for the people, instead of just soaking in.

"THAT'S IT!" Just like that! "That's what we need! Aw, good! Good!"

Telephone. Right! "PR division…. Who's in charge…? Right. Here's what we're doin', and we want you to come and line a lake."

And they guy's like, "Well, you don't understand, it's not something we *do*."

"Well, yeah, but listen, it's for Ringo Starr, from The Beatles and all."

And that's got the guy. "Oh, yeah, okay, that's different! We'll get some PR outta that one."

So they send a guy over to Tittenhurst Park, and he's like, "Oh, God, what're you doin'?"

We said, "Well, we're tryin' to build a lake."

"God. Right. Okay." So they measure everything with surveyors, angles, math, on and on, then, "Yeah, okay, we can do it."

"Yeah! All right!"

"It's gonna cost, like...."

"Aw, just do it." We don't care. It doesn't matter.

So he comes back in a couple of weeks with all these trucks, with *great big* rolls of this heavy dive suit-like rubber, and these really weird-looking machines. A big bunch of guys start rolling it out, and these machines heat the rolls and seal all the rubber. It stinks like hell! *Acres* of it! There's other private estates around, and a lot of the Queen's land around it as well, in Royal Ascot.

"We shouldn't've dug so much." They go all the way around, and it's all lined.

"Okay! Off we go! More water!" Yeah! Great, man! We turn on the water, sssssssss, water everywhere, fill it up.

We go back the next morning.... "You look first!"

"No, you look!"

"Oh, I don't wanna look!"

"No, you look."

I go, "Okay.... Still there!"

"Yeah! Water! Congratulations!"

"Now what?"

We need fish. Gotta have fish. It's a lake, you know. But you can't just go down to the local fish store, you have to phone fish farm type people. They came with tankers full of perch and God knows what else. Fortunately we've still got the bloody log road in. So they come on down and hose it all out, great big hoses with just fish! Fabulous! Lovely. There were maybe 100,000 fish.

A couple days later, bloop, bloop, bloop...fish are dying! The place is stinking! What? There's millions of fish everywhere, dead, just floating around. One of me mates says, "What's the problem here?"

I said, "Oh, God, I don't know." The mess was on our hands. We were trying to get it together before Ringo got back in town.

There's a local university, so we phoned them, "Got a fish problem here." So they send over one of their biologists. This guy goes, "What'd you all do?"

"Well, we just threw all these fish in."

He says, "Look. There's no food. There's no ecosystem…it's rubber! There's no oxygen in here. It's just not happening. This won't work."

"Aw, man!"

We get the local farmers' lads and poachers and people with bloody nets to get rid of all the dead fish. Took forever.

And then the biologist gave us a list. We had to buy all these weeds, and put in solid dirt and mud and all, and all the weeds have to start growing. It was a pretty complex gig.

This time, we just tried a couple of fish. We got clever. We put a pen off the side and threw some fish in, and kept an eye on 'em for a couple of days, "Hello? You all right?" Give 'em some food and stuff. And it seemed to work. 'Cause you've gotta have a natural environment for acres of water.

"Okay, more fish! There we go!" And a couple of dozen died, but nothing serious, nothing like the first time.

When Ringo came back he thought it was fabulous. "Nice lake!" The dogs and the kids loved it. You might hear people say that John put in the lake, but he didn't. A lot of people didn't even know—and still don't know—that Ringo bought the estate from John. Or that *we* put in the lake.

Fistfight with Rod Stewart

I was still going back and forth to London, still had the Apple house there. I was in a fight with Rod Stewart in London once. Rod had just hit big time, just played The Speakeasy. We were all at Tramps, and Hilary (Ringo's personal manager) was there with a beautiful woman. Rod was pissed as a parrot that night, and he started saying some stuff to Hilary's lady. Next thing I know he's got Hilary by the neck of his shirt. Well, that's one of my guys! So I went over and grabbed Rod and said, "Bug off!" Next thing you know all of his guys come over, ready to tear me off, then they see it's me. And I know them and I say, "Hang on, let's calm down here," and they said "Why'd you go and do that?" and I told them he attacked my guy. We got it all straightened out.

Son of Dracula Movie

There was so much product from Apple and the former Beatles, and so many projects going on. Ringo had started Apple Films; it was kind of his toy. He had an editing room at Apple in the basement. And in 1973/74 we were doing a movie with Harry Nilsson. He was cast as Dracula in one of Ringo's favorite projects, *Son of Dracula*. I think it was *Count Downe* or *Young Dracula* in the U.K. To my knowledge it's never been released. Nobody's ever heard of it. But it was a great movie! In some ways. If anybody ever sees a pirated edition…there's a couple sneaking around.

All Ringo's mates are in it: Harry Nilsson, Peter Frampton, John Bonham, Keith Moon, Joey Molland from Badfinger. I was in charge of the booze. We had a bar everywhere we went. We had one on the set, and if we were on location, we'd book the local pub, give 'em 1000 quid and it'd be an open bar for the crew and everyone. Ringo was producer, and to him that meant he did everything and paid for everything. Like a host. It was a moving party around southern England 24 hours a day—hash, grass, coke.

But the movie's sooooo bad. Me and Kenny did the driving. Any scene with a car in it was me or Kenny. That's me driving the hearse at the beginning. It's a rented American car, a Buick, from the '60s.

The movie's interiors are all in a warehouse on the Thames next to The Tower of London, in the dock area. Ringo leased the warehouse and hired set builders. For the exteriors Ringo rented a castle southwest of London, in the country.

So really nobody's every seen it—never. But, okay, I have a copy. When Kenny flew in for my 57th birthday party this year, I just popped it in one afternoon after we'd had a couple beers. He said, "What's that?" The music starts and the titles, and he's all, "WHAT? NO! What the…? How'd you get ahold of that?"

A friend of mine knows I worked for this lot, and he just turned up one day and said, "Here." It was a gift. He found it on the Internet. I think it's pirated. But it's a good copy. Some of it gets a bit grainy, but generally speaking it's quite a good copy. The movie's a good giggle. But making it really was a good time.

An Irish Gypsy Vacation

I'd been all over the world doing business for Hilary Gerrard, Ringo's business manager—moving papers, bills, diamonds, all sorts of stuff. I had to go to Amsterdam, then down to Monte Carlo, and over to the Virgin Islands.... I was taking pouches around of paperwork, transferring funds, business type stuff. Keeping the taxman away, you know.

I get back to Heathrow and I'm shattered, jet lagged. I get off, come through customs, and there's one of our guys waiting for me, Peter. I can't wait to get home. He says, "Here's another ticket. You've gotta go somewhere now. You've still got your suitcase. Here's a pouch, let's go."

"Oh...no!"

He said, "Don't worry, you're going first class."

I always traveled first class so I said, "Oh, yeah, big deal."

He took me down to domestic flights. All right. It was Aer Lingus, Irish airlines, which goes to Ireland but also does a lot of stops around England. So I get on the plane, where I'm allowed to open up the pouch so I can find out what I'm supposed to do at the other end. It's just a little note from Ringo, saying, "Have a good time, Bryan. Somebody will meet you in Dublin Airport. Thanks, Ringo." There was a big wad of cash...what's this?

The plane lands, I get off, and there's a guy on the concourse with a sign with my name on it, "Rooney." Oh, that's me! "Yo!" Like there's not a million Rooneys getting off a plane in Dublin. It's this old farmer, in Wellingtons and an old jacket all torn. "'Ow are ya." Typical Irishman, he says, "Let's go to the bar."

I said, "I'm with you." We drink a coupla pints of Guinness.

So I says, "Where're we goin'?"

He says, "We're going to my farm."

They're not gonna stick me in a farmhouse for a bleeding week? I'll kill myself; I'll kill someone.

He wouldn't tell me what was happening. So we get into an old battered Land Rover and off we go out of Dublin, down the road into the countryside. And we get to this guy's farm. It's all tumbled, beautifully painted, but falling, 'cause it's been there since the 15th century or something. He's got sheep, a couple of llamas, all sorts of stuff there.

I says, "Okay, cool. Do you want some dinner? I'm kinda beat."

He says, "Well no. Hang on. Let me explain. Come here."

We go around into the barnyard and he goes into one of the barns and comes out with this really big horse, like a cart horse, big with shaggy feet. Not quite a Clydesdale, it was more like a Shire horse. And he gets all this tackle out, leather harnesses and stuff. And he puts it on the horse and opens up the two gates to the barn and backs the horse in. What's going on here? I need another drink. This is nuts.

And he puts the horse into the shafts of this beautiful hand-painted gypsy caravan. Have you ever seen a gypsy caravan? Little chimney on it. He says, kinda gruff, "This is your holiday, your vacation. It was paid for by some office in…London. Sign here." He either didn't know who The Beatles were, or didn't care.

I says, "I don't know nothing about…."

"You don't need to. It's for tourists like you. Americans."

"But I'm Irish! English! I'm from Liverpool!"

He goes, "Whatever. English. It's all the same. Sign here."

"I don't believe this. I don't know…."

"The horse knows where it's going. *Don't* worry. Just get on and go, 'Giddup,' like that."

"Wha—?"

"Look, there's food in there, there's a little stove, little wood fireplace. There's a cooler, there's a bunch of drinks that they've ordered for you—gin, scotch, bourbon—*American* bourbon. Ice. I've even got ice." Which was like a huge job to get ice in that day and age, it's unheard of. God knows how he got ice, because people didn't have icemakers.

I climb up on the caravan, way up, 'cause it's on springs and stuff. He gets a cushion and throws it at me; I'm the stupid foreigner.

"Right, see you in three weeks."

"Three weeks!"

He's really gruff now, he says, "Don't worry, we know where you're going. Any problems, the number's on the piece of paper. Go." Because he didn't wanna bother with making me dinner. God!

So, "Giddup!" And the horse starts, one hoof at a time. Gedunk, gedunk, really slowly. Out the farm drive, gets to the road—can't call it a main road 'cause it's just a little country road with a hedge, trees. And the horse just hangs a left. Gedunk, gedunk. After about 10 minutes I see you don't have to steer because it just goes, it just does it.

There's a little door into the back. I go in: This is cool. I go sit up front again, I put the reins on me knees, like a professional. And off I go on this horse and gypsy caravan that Ringo's put together for me. And we just go down the country lanes.

About an hour later we come to this little village. Gedunk, gedunk. Then the horse just stops…right outside the pub. It's the truth! This is the horse's route, it knows what it's doing. It just stops, no breaks or anything.

So I climb down and someone peeks out the window 'cause they'd heard the horse pull up, and a little teenage guy comes running out, "Hey, Mr. Rooney! Welcome! Welcome! We've been expecting you! Come on in. We've got your dinner."

"What…? Where…?"

And he goes, "I'll take care of that. I'll put the horse in the field there for you."

Apparently what happens is, everywhere you go, they expect ya. And they just park it up for you next to the inn, take all the tackle off and let the horse go and eat the grass, and they give it some oats. They put the whole trip together. They still do it to this day.

They know how far the horse can go per day, so they know when it's going to stop in the evening, they know what village it's going to stop at. And they arrange for the horse to be taken into a field. And then you go in the pub and have a *great* meal and a couple of pints, and they're all going, "Here you go!"

I'm going, "This is cool! Well done!"

And then they take you back to your caravan and they've built you a little fire, and you take a coupla guys with you and give 'em a drinks, and they're all happy.

I slept in my little caravan. It's got a beautiful little bed, and it's got a handwoven Irish wool quilt, feather pillows. Brilliant! And a little fire venting out the little chimney. Sleep warm all night. Then you get up in the morning and they give you an Irish breakfast, put the horse and caravan back together for you, and they just wave you goodbye.

I'm like, "I'm king of the castle!" Gedunk, gedunk. You're not going fast. If you wanted to go a bit faster you could flick the rein and the horse'd look at you and go a bit faster for about 5 minutes, then it was like, "Piss off" and back to slow. The horse knows its own pace. It knows the next village is a certain distance a way, it's done it a million times. And it goes in a big loop.

So the trip was thanks to Ringo telling the Apple office to put it together for me. And I was so refreshed when I was done. Nothing exotic, but it was a *great* vacation. And as I said, they still do it today. Jill and I were over there with Gemma and we rented cottages and I noticed a couple of those caravans going down the road. Beautiful Irish folk art.

Working for Ringo's Manager Hilary Gerrard

Around the time when Hilary Gerrard—incredible guy—became Ringo's business manager, Kenny moved on to work with Greg Lake of Emerson, Lake, and Palmer. It would probably have been about 1975. We'd been at Tittenhurst with Ringo, and Greg Lake's beautiful 16th century mansion was just around the corner. We knew his people, and we all used to go to The Nag's Head because it was such a beautiful place. There were pubs everywhere, but The Nag's Head was kind of a central meeting place.

One of Greg Lake's guys told Kenny that Greg was looking for a personal manager/assistant, like Kenny was doing for Ringo. I guess

Kenny was getting bored sitting around at Tittenhurst every day. I got to do all the travel because I was the gopher. Ringo wanted Kenny with him, so Kenny didn't go anywhere. I got to go to exotica while Kenny had another day at the bloody mansion.

Greg made Kenny an offer which was quite good, because Greg was really very interested in hiring Kenny. They were going to be going to Switzerland and wanted Kenny to go with them. So Kenny did.

Hilary Gerrard was Ringo's business manager, and I was still working for and paid by Apple, assisting Ringo, working under Hilary. I was getting paid by Apple but I was tied to Ringo and Kenny, then Hilary. I still did my usual routine. They never really brought anybody else in to replace Kenny. We just carried on. Hilary's still Ringo's manager to this day.

Barbara was Ringo's personal secretary/assistant, paying the nannies, gardeners. She was very good. She'd been around a long time. And her husband Michael O'Donnell was in charge of Ringo's studio and all the recording stuff, the equipment. Anything to do with technical stuff. They lived at a cottage at the estate. Joan took care of the Apple side of Ringo's business.

For a while, because of England's tax system, Ringo officially lived in Monte Carlo, in the south of France. So every so often Ringo, his girlfriend Nancy Andrews, and I went to Monte Carlo. Ringo had a beautiful apartment there. We were shopping, being invited to parties, going to the casino, hanging out on the yachts in the harbor. It's Monte Carlo! It's incredible.

Photos

Tittenhurst Park in the early 1970s after Ringo Starr bought the estate from John Lennon: Ringo's assistant Kenny Smith, Kenny's assistant Bryan Rooney, and St. James Infirmary drummer Pete Rooney.

Ringo Starr's recording studio at Tittenhurst Park: Bryan Rooney, Ringo, and recording studio manager Mike O'Donnell.

Photos

Publicity poster for 1974's *Son of Dracula* (released by Apple Films, ©1974). Bryan Rooney drives the hearse at the beginning and several other vehicles, and ran the movie sets' bars.

Bryan Rooney when he moved "Out West" to Los Angeles in 1975.

Photos

Bryan's then-girlfriend Jill's 21st birthday party at Mick and Melody Coles's home in West Hollywood, California, moments before Bryan smashed his face into the cake.

87

BackStage with Bryan Rooney

The Who's drummer Keith Moon with Bryan Rooney (filling in for Keith's assistant Dougal Butler) in hip blue velvet 3-piece suits at the King's Head Pub in Santa Monica, California, around Christmastime 1976.

Photos

Bryan and Jill's Rooney's Wedding at Ringo Starr's home above Sunset Boulevard in Beverly Hills, California, February 1977: Ringo's girlfriend Nancy Andrews, Maid of Honor Debbie East, Jill and Bryan Rooney, Best Man Ringo Starr, Actress/Minister Sally Kirkland. Because Sally Kirkland performed the marriage ceremony, the wedding was written up in *Variety* magazine.

Just Married: Jill and Bryan Rooney with Best Man Ringo Starr.

Ringo Starr catching the garter Bryan threw: Donna Summer's lighting director Keith Robertson, Ringo's manager Hilary Gerrard, Tam Smith, Donna Summer's tour manager Mick Coles, Ringo's lawyer Bruce Grakal, German surrealist artist and Donna Summer's boyfriend Peter Muhldorfer, and Ringo. Bryan was already missing one front tooth when he met Jill, and lost the rest at a riot at a Donna Summer concert in Milan.

Some of Bryan and Jill Rooney's wedding guests: Donna Summer's secretary Patricia Naderhoff, Ringo Starr's manager Hilary Gerrard, Donna Summer's tour manager Mick Coles, German surrealist artist and Donna Summer's boyfriend Peter Muhldorfer, and Donna Summer.

Bryan and Jill Rooney at Barney's Beanery one Halloween.

L'Ermitage Hotel in Beverly Hills one Christmas: Dale Kamai, The Who's bassist John Entwistle and his then-girlfriend Maxine Harlow, and Jill and Bryan Rooney.

Photos

Some of Donna Summer's band, staff, and road crew with Muhammad Ali in Las Vegas c. 1976. Back row 3rd from left Donna's synthesizer player Virgil Weber, Muhammad Ali, unknown woman, Donna's percussionist Bob Conti, unknown man, Donna's secretary Patricia Naderhoff; in front of Muhammad Ali is Donna's manager Susan Munao, kneeling next to Susan is Donna's backup singer Carlene Williams; Donna Summer is kneeling in front wearing boxing gloves.

Donna Summer's road crew members Phil Demonte and
Bryan Rooney, percussionist Bob Conti, and roadie Frankie Heather.

Donna Summer's production manager Bryan Rooney and tour manager Mick Coles with concert promoters in The Philippines.

Mick Coles and Bryan Rooney in The Philippines while on tour with Donna Summer.

Donna Summer's lighting director Chris Dale, Jill Rooney, and production manager Bryan Rooney on tour with Donna Summer at the MGM Grand in Las Vegas.

Donna Summer's tour manager Bryan Rooney, lighting director Keith Robertson, and road crew member Bob Pope.

Bryan Rooney, Scorpions tour manager Bob Adcock, and Eurythmics manager Kenny Smith at Los Angeles's Sunset Marquee in the early 1980s.

Photos

Susan, Bryan, and Diane Rooney reunited in Los Angeles in the mid-1980s.

London 1975

Bryan Rooney filming *BackStage* video segments in 2005.

Kenny Smith at Bryan Rooney's 57th birthday party at Bryan's home near Los Angeles, June 2006.

BackStage's Vince Falzone at Bryan Rooney's 57th birthday party.

Los Angeles

In 1975 I was still traveling back and forth from England to everywhere as an assistant to Ringo's manager Hilary Gerrard. Everyone would go, "Wow!" But it was getting kind of boring. I still wanted to be involved with something, want-ed to do something different.

Mark Clarke, my old school friend and from the original band that we went to London with, St. James Infirmary, reappeared one day. "Oh, hello! What's happenin', man?"

He was the guy who'd really got me started in the whole business. It's all like a big circle. A really bent, twisted circle. After all that madness with St. James Infirmary, then on the road with Procol Harum, then Apple, I should've just hit him and said, "You got me into this, you lunatic!"

But we got talking again, and he said "Well, we're putting a band together."

"Oh, yeah, who's that, then?"

"Well, it's gonna be me," he was a great, great bass player, "Jerry Shirley, the drummer from Humble Pie, Joey Molland, the guitarist from Badfinger, and Pete Wood from Pink Floyd, the keyboard player," who was a session guy forever, an incredible artist. That was the new band, Natural Gas. "We're goin' to America. We need somebody to come with us, to take care of it." A lot of record companies would rent the Apple studio for their bands, so the musicians ended up getting to know each other. Natural Gas wanted to go to America to shop their record to Warner Brothers, Capitol, etc. In the mid-1970s there was a shift in the music industry, and everybody wanted to go to L.A.—Humble Pie, Small Faces, everybody.

"Oh, that sounds all right.... Yeah."

A couple months or so later when Natural Gas had it together, I told Ringo. There was nothing nasty or anything about it, it was just, "Oh, okay! Carry on." That's how generous he was. "Anything happens, give me a call."

So I started working for Natural Gas's management company as their road manager. It was my first time as an actual road manager. We put it all together—the equipment, the driving, the hotels, and flew to Los Angeles.

We stayed at the Riot House, which is the Hyatt House on Sunset Strip, opposite the House of Blues. It's still there now, though I don't know if it's still a Hyatt. Everybody called it the Riot House, because *every* band who was coming to L.A. stayed there. It was near all the clubs, and just a short limo ride to The Forum. The Who, Zeppelin, whoever was in town stayed at the Riot House. It was like a riot every weekend.

Someone Else Tumbling Down Stairs

So there's a whole bunch of us in The Riot House—Hyatt House—on Sunset Strip. Zeppelin's in town, so the place is mobbed with groupies, non-groupies, anybody, everybody.

The lobby had a big flight of stairs that led upstairs. I'm sitting down in the bar on the other side of the lobby with a coupla Zeppelin's crew, having a quiet drink in the corner, when there's all this racket and shouting.

Mick Hinton, Bonham's drum roadie, was a great guy, and a *big*, big man. Mick comes staggering into the bar with his shirt all asunder, a black eye, and a bruise here and there.

All we crew were like, "What's happenin'? Who did it? We'll get 'im!" 'Cause everyone sticks up for each other.

Mick is going, "That's it! I quit!"

I said, "What's the problem?"

"Ay, it's the bloody lunatic, Bonham!"

"What?"

"He's just kicked me down the fuckin' stairs!"

I said, "Oh, no! I've been there!"

He says, "Right?"

I says, "George Harrison did that to me way back!"

Bonham had got annoyed with the guy over something stupid, like he didn't have enough drumsticks, or they were the wrong size, and kicked him down this flight of stairs, down into the lobby and the bar area. Mick just tumbled down.

Bonham's at the top screaming, "You stupid git!" And Mick comes into the bar and we're ready for a big fight, thinking somebody's been hurting him—and it was actually his own guy!

Bonham storms off somewhere to throw another TV out the bedroom onto the canopies or something. That was the big sport, especially for Keith Moon. It was hysterical, but it was really dangerous to walk below! So we patch Mick up and give him a coupla cognacs. He's all right, so we're all right. He and Bonham make up again. They're like kids, "I'm sorry," "It's okay."

It's all another day in the office.... Stuff like that happens, and you deal with it.

A Redhead Catches My Eye

In September 1975 I'm kind of stuck in L.A.'s Hyatt House, as Natural Gas's management is paying me and covering my room and board. But I'm an Englishman stuck in America.

One day I'm looking out my Hyatt window, and opposite the Hyatt House is a little strip mall with clothing boutiques, a smoke shop, stuff like that. It's the corner where the House of Blues is now.

I was looking over at the strip mall, and I see this girl in a boutique who is *really* beautiful. I thought, "What's all that?"

So I had a quick drink—Dutch courage—and scampered across Sunset Strip, nearly getting killed 'cause there was no crosswalk there. I go into the boutique, The Real Thing, which is a costumer for rock 'n' roll bands, selling leather clothing for them to wear on stage. Good place for it, across from Hyatt House. I go, "'Ello. My name is Bryan. How are you? What's happenin'?"

She said, "I'm Jill. Are you lookin' to buy somethin'?"

I said, "No, no, I just saw you…. I'm stayin' at the hotel, and I thought I'd come over and say hello and take you to lunch." Liverpool people are very smooth, you know? No messing about—straight in.

She goes, "Oh, I'd really like to. But I can't leave because the guy who owns this place has gone for the day, and I don't have the keys to lock it up."

"Oh, okay. Well, never mind…. Nice to see ya." And I came back over to the hotel.

Then I thought, hang on! I can do something. I got in my car—well, it was the band's car, it was leased. I went to the nearest hardware store and bought a length of chain and a padlock.

I went back to the boutique and said, "Right. It's okay, we can go for lunch, we'll just go here." There were a few little trendy restaurants, wine bar type things, in the same mini mall. It wasn't like I was taking her far. "I'll lock it up for you. Come on out." I put the chain through the door handles, put the padlock on: Closed! And I took her to lunch.

We started dating. So 1975 and 1976 I was in and out of Los Angeles doing various things for various people. Some of me mates in London would call and say they needed an extra hand for a couple of weeks, or maybe needed someone in Monterey. Some guys would say, "We need a body. We need do go up to Frisco and do a show." I'd go and make a couple of bucks.

Jill had had several apartments, and whenever I was in town I'd stay with her, you know, a coupla nights here, or a week here or there. Every time I came back into town, I'd find her. She moved a few times, and I would never know where she'd gone. But she still went to The Rainbow, The Roxy, all the same clubs. I'd find her again, take her out for dinner, and then we'd go down the beach…. And then I'd just disappear again.

Then I'd come back and she's moved. I'd have to go and track her down. I'd just find her.

She'd get annoyed with me. "Oh, God, he's gone again." I'd just disappear into the wild blue yonder, and that was that. She wasn't one to hang around and cry over it, she just carried on with her own thing. I was still a laggard, a gypsy. Being a hooligan, tramping around with the lads, you know, party here, party there.

But whenever I *found* her, she was always there for me. She was always really kind, and always gave me a bed so I didn't have to deal with hotels or anything. And I got to know her mother.... She was a gorgeous, gorgeous girl.

Working for Ringo/Apple Again

There I was, yet again, in the middle of more trouble. Within a few months of arriving in L.A. Natural Gas got a record deal with Private Stock Records, I think. They made an album in 1976 called *Natural Gas*... and it didn't do anything. It just plummeted. The album wasn't a disaster —it was quite a good album—but nobody really got into it. It just didn't sell, and they gave up on it. There were some ego issues, some fighting too. So Natural Gas broke up. Joey and Jerry stayed in L.A. and reformed Badfinger. There were still some bits and pieces to take care of while the band was in the process of breaking up, and some little jobs to keep me around until the management had something else for me.

But I was getting tired of the bits and pieces of work. In those days everybody pretty much was concentrated in the same place: on Sunset Strip, at the same clubs, same restaurants. It's kind of inevitable that at one point or another you're gonna bounce into somebody you know— Ringo, Keith Moon, John Bonham. Everybody's in L.A. Harry Nilsson had come back too. We all congregated, like birds fly south seasonally. And you knew when somebody was in town 'cause the word was out on the streets, and the girls'd tell ya. Ringo was based in L.A. by then, though he was still a "resident" of Monte Carlo, so went back and forth.

One day there Ringo was, sitting at a table at a nice restaurant called La Dome. It'd been about a little less than a year or so since I'd seen him.

He says, "Come on, sit down! Right. What're you doin'?"

I said, "Oh, not working much, bits and pieces, nothing serious really."

He said, "Oh, well, come on back then, and help me out!"

"Okay, yeah. That'd be nice." He's got a real nice house in Beverly Hills, up off Sunset Boulevard, above all the rabble. So I was back with Ringo, on Apple's payroll. I started schlepping Ringo around L.A., taking care of him, make sure he got everywhere he needed to go.

Filling in for Keith Moon's Assistant

Back in L.A., 1976, I went to the world famous Rainbow on Sunset Boulevard next to The Roxy. It was the hub of lunacy.

I'd been out of town in Caracas, Venezuela, on business for Ringo, and had just came back in. I was really tired and went over to The Rainbow for a meal—they have great food—and a drink, as per usual. I'm sitting downstairs, then finished eating and I needed to go the bathroom, which is upstairs.

Also upstairs is another little room which is kind of exclusive. It's not really open to the public, it's more or less who you are or who you know. I know they're gonna let me in, 'cause they know me. Bear the bouncer was a great guy. *Big* guy. His name was Oso, which means Bear. I took him on the road with me later, with Donna Summer, as security. He said, "Who are you? Oh, Bryan! Welcome back!"

I wander into this room, and at the back booth, lo and behold, there's Ringo, Harry Nilsson, Keith Moon, and Keith's personal assistant, Dougal Butler.

Keith Moon's nickname "Moon the Loon" was well-earned. He graduated from The College of Total Lunacy. I mean, if you're gonna be a lunatic, he was the man to look up to.

Keith's personal assistant Dougal comes hurling over to me. "Bryan! What're you doin'?"

"Oh, I just got back in. I'm tired."

He says, "Gotta help me."

"Doin' what?" I get suspicious. "What do you mean?"

"I've *got* to get back to London."

I says, "Well, get on an aeroplane like everybody else. That's fair."

"No, no, my wife's havin' problems, she's just about to deliver a baby; I've *gotta* get back."

"Well…go!"

He said, "Well, I can't leave Keith Moon on his own," because everyone knows that's tantamount to murder, 'cause the guy just needs control. There's gotta be somebody with him all the time.

Dougal says, "Oh, come on," and he gives me another cognac or something, and he talks me into it. Bastard!

"Yeah, okay, I'll do it."

Liverpool has a different point of view on things, and so people from there do too. Something happens and it's "Oh, okay," when everybody else would go, "But that's nuts! You shouldn't do it like that!" People from Liverpool just go blithely on the way, "Oh well, this is cool." It's an attitude, but it isn't like, "Ew. Get. Off. Me." It's like, "Oh, yeah, okay! Let's do it."

Dougal says, "Good man! Here's the valet ticket for the car. There's Keith. When he's ready, get him home." I'm thinking by "home" he meant a hotel around the corner somewhere. Then he says, "Oh, okay, gotta go! I need to split!"

He's got his passport, he's got an overnight bag, and he's gone! He *knew* someone was gonna come along.

I was a sucker! I felt like an idiot. Dougal just splits, goes, leaves me the bloody valet ticket and that's the end of it. Nice one! Clever.

I wander over to Keith, and he says, "Ah, Bryan!" Ringo and Harry Nilsson are with him and they're like, "Yeah!," "Great!," and "How's it goin', man?"

I said, "I'm okay. Keith, I'm in charge of you from now on, until your lad gets back."

He says, "What?"

I says, "Well, Dougal's gone to London."

"What? Didn't tell me."

"Well, his wife's pregnant, their baby's due any minute, so he had to get outta here, and he put me in charge."

Keith just goes, "Oh! Okay, that's cool. No problem." He doesn't care, as long as he's got somebody to lean on. You're not going to have an interview or have someone ask for your resume in these situations, you just get, "Oh, okay, man!" I sit down at their booth.

It's very dark in there. A couple hours later the lights go on 'cause they're closing up and all that. Keith says, "O-kay! Let's go! Time to go!"

Ringo stands up. He was wearing one of his regular black velvet suits, with nice handmade boots. Ringo's a sharp dude, always looked cool. I was wearing jeans and a really nice silk shirt, handmade by my girlfriend. Smart but casual.

Keith stands up, and I suddenly realize he's got a Nazi uniform on. Good God! He was sitting down in the booth, and I wasn't paying attention to what he was wearing. Here he's got a Swastika band on his upper arm, jackboots, and a German tank commander's helmet with "SS" and a skull on it. And a belt with a Luger. It was a model, but looked like a real gun.

Oh, brilliant. But I said, "Okay. Come on. Downstairs."

I give the valet guy the ticket, thinking Keith's gonna have a Mercedes, or another regular, standard luxury vehicle.

The guy pulls out of the parking lot behind the bloody Roxy with this... *long* car, seemed like 38-foot! It was an Excalibur, a completely custom car, American made. If you've never seen one, they're *huge*. The bonnet—the hood—had a V-16 or something. It looked like the old Mercedes convertible touring car Hitler used to scoot around Berlin in.

I've been in some fancy cars, but nothing like this. The roof's down: It's a convertible. And it's blue glitter, not a dark blue, but a bright Liberace blue. The tires were white-walled, the leather seats were white.

Oh my.... Ah, good God! So...right. "Get in."

I get Keith in the back seat, lock the door and everything, and get in the driver's seat. "Right. Where're we goin'?"

He says, "Okay…! Well, I live in Broad Beach."

Hang on! Whoa! Time out! "That's in Malibu!"

He says, "Yeah! I've got a house in Malibu on the beach." Malibu is northwest of L.A. My girlfriend and I went to Malibu to play, to hang around and go on the beach and stuff. So I knew where it was, and I knew it was a long way!

"Oh, God!"

"Look," Keith says as he writes down the address, "When you get there, this is the code, 'cause you have to code in the gate and all that. Let's go!"

"Okay…." So I'm off down Sunset, and in those days Sunset's like a zoo on the way down to Pacific Coast Highway. It's not an easy drive, and at 3 in the morning it's seriously dark. I'm in this *huge* machine with a steering wheel that's bigger than me, and my passenger in the back seat is dressed up like a Nazi.

I'm driving this thing, and I'm trying to get used to it, 'cause the first time in a car you have to get into the swing of it. We get down to Pacific Coast Highway and there's the ocean…nice! I turn onto Pacific Coast and we have to go north to get to Malibu and then Broad Beach.

As we're driving along, Keith hits the 8-track, and he's playing "Land of Hope and Glory," *daaaaahhh*! It's almost like "The National Anthem," *aaaaaaaaaah, doo da* DAAAAAAAAAH!

Oh, and he's hitting me with his whip. He's got this whip like you use on horses. I go, "Stop it! I'm trying to drive, you idiot!"

He goes, "Aw, it's great, man! Look at the stars!"

"Yeah. Great. Brilliant."

And sure enough—had to happen—whoop whoop whoop, *maaaa*, MAAAAAA! Lights flashing. That's all I bloody need: The cops, at 3 in the morning, with me driving this *huge* car, and a Nazi in the back seat whipping me.

I go, "Keith, stop it!"

The cops want me to pull over, obviously, so I pull over, and they pull over. They keep a distance, like they're thinking, "This is a bit dodgy." Then on the speaker system from the police car is, "Get out of your car."

"Ahhh...it's okay, man, it's cool." At this point I'm holding my hands up in the air, 'cause I know the cops' system.

The next thing I know, Keith pulls his mock Luger. That's it. I'm dead.

So the cops pull their guns, and there's this standoff. For a minute in time, there's this Nazi tank commander with a whip and a Luger, and 2 scared-looking cops who didn't know *what* was happening, and a driver with his hands in the air. Aw, man!

So I think hard, and pick the only way I'm gonna live through this business. I turn 'round, *smack!*, and plant a punch on Keith Moon's jaw. He falls out the car, 'cause it's an open convertible, and is laying on the deck, the trunk, in full Nazi uniform.

I get out the car and get on my knees and I'm crawling towards the cops. They're like, "What's goin' on? What's happenin'?"

I said, "It's okay! I'm his chauffer."

"What?"

"That guy is Keith Moon, the drummer from The Who."

And the younger cop is going, "Ohhhh, sure." Then, "Really?"

"Honestly! Don't worry. He's down. The gun's a wooden model."

They're shaking, and I'm shaking, and Keith's groaning, and he starts screaming, "SHOOT THE PIGS!"

I shout, "Man! Stop it!"

The cops come closer, and I said, "Look," and I gave 'em the gun, and I tapped it out. "Here, here's the gun, it's wooden. It's a model. It can't kill you. It doesn't do anything."

Then, in a flash of genius, I said, "We've just been in town to a fancy, crazy, rock 'n' roll dress ball…. He won first place for his costume. He won a magnum of champagne, which he drank. He's had too much, and I'm tryin' to get 'im home to Broad Beach."

The cops look at 'im, poke him around a bit, and they're going, "Really!"

"Well, that's the story, that's what happened," I said. "Look. Tell you what you can do. Let me get him back in the car, and then escort me to Broad Beach, 'cause I've never been there."

The cops are all hesitant. I said, "Keith Moon! Famous rock…?"

The younger guy's going, "Oh, yeah!" Of course, Keith didn't have ID, not unless it was an SS-stamped Fuhrer badge or something. None of them carried ID then. It was just, "You know me. I'm Ringo."

So, fair enough that the cops are hesitating. But…I'd bamboozled them! They throw Mooney in the back of the bloody car, drive 'round in front of me, and turn on lights and escort me all the way! This is cool!

We get to Broad Beach, to his neighborhood, and I've got the gate code. The cops do a u-turn and I wave and say, "What station're you at? I'll send you some albums and shit."

"Oh, okay!" By now I'm the best of friends with them. So they give me their badge numbers and their names and everything and where they are located, headquarters are and all that.

"Give me a week or so. Thanks for the escort! Really appreciate it."

"Well, okay, no problem, Bryan." It's like they're thinking, "Good man! That's what we like to see, a good upright standing citizen" or whatever it was. I did send them albums, whatever was in the house, I think it was *The Who: Live at Leeds*.

The gate opens, and I drive in and try to find his house. There's 4 houses in a row, and his is in the middle. When I find the right house number I just abandon the car, drag him out, riffle through his pockets and find a set of keys, open the front door, and kick him in. I was like wood at this point, 'cause remember I'd just flown in from Venezuela. I fall in after him. He goes somewhere, to a bedroom or God knows where. I see a sofa and collapse.

I'm asleep. And then, instantaneously, *bang bang bang bang*.

I wake up and it's daylight, dawn, and I don't know where I am. It's all a blur. Then, oh, no, I'm in Keith Moon's house. All right. Okay, cool.

But what's that noise? BANG BANG BANG BANG BANG!

So I go up the stairs to open the front door, and this guy in his dressing gown goes, "Are you with that lunatic?"

"Yeah..., I think so...."

He said stiffly, "I live there." That's next door. "I just had people knocking on *my* door telling me there's a dead German washed up from a submarine."

"Awwww...." Here we go! What the hell did I do this for?

It's a big house. I go over to the other side of the house, to the balcony, and look down. There's Keith Moon with a bottle of cognac, his tank commander hat all askew, flat out on the beach. When I'd gone to sleep he'd grabbed a bottle and taken a walk on the beach and collapsed.

Oh, God, now what? Well, he's too big for me to move, 'cause he was a big, squat, heavy guy in those days. Big.

So I get a blanket, a coupla pillows, and a book. He had a lot of books there—very well-read guy. I go down the steps—*a lot* of steps—to the beach and go over to him.

There's joggers practically tripping over him, dogs barking at him, seagulls landing on his head, and God knows what. I shoo them away, lay the blanket down over him to hide his uniform, put a pillow under his head, and take his bloody tank helmet off. I pat him down to make sure there's no Luger hidden anywhere, or a submachine gun or hand grenades or God knows what. He could have smuggled down a Howitzer. I settled down on the beach and went, "Ahhhh, right."

I turned 'round and here's the other house next door, on the other side of us from where the guy (later on he told me he was a publisher) had come to knock on the door. Steve McQueen and Ali MacGraw are sitting on their balcony, trying to have breakfast with all this commotion on the beach, in their little private community...with a Nazi who's reportedly just been washed up off a submarine.

Why me, Lord?

Obviously I had to stay until Keith came to eventually. He staggered upstairs, had a coffee, got changed, and demanded to go to the local pub. And off we went.

That was just the first of several weeks of Keith Moon. I shoulda known better.

There's a photo of us on the wall at the King's Head, the English pub in Santa Monica, on Santa Monica Boulevard and Ocean. It's a great place. We're both in blue velvet suits. Very stylish.

Keith had to go back to London because The Who were doing something and he had to go to the studio in London. I'd kept in touch with Dougal, whose wife had had the baby. I had things I had to do here, and I had to stay in L.A. anyway. So I arranged for Dougal to get him at the other end and take him to the studio or whatever.

Keith gave me a check for 10 grand for the weeks I'd spent with 'im. On the memo line he wrote "choreography." When I took the check to the bank, it didn't clear. I've still got it here somewhere....

In London Keith stayed in Harry Nilsson's apartment. Less than a year later, he OD'd there...and died, God bless 'im. It was the same place that Mama Cass died a few years earlier. For Keith it was too much booze and pills, the usual for that crowd. Uppers, downers. It wasn't deliberate, wasn't a suicide for sure. He drowned in his own vomit.

That was very, very heavy.

Tying the Knot at Ringo's Home

Jill and I moved in together eventually, when I was just bouncing around, doing little mini-tours for people, as well as stuff for people connected to the label Natural Gas had been with before they broke up. I was getting the car paid for, etc.

Then I was back with Ringo again, so I was stable, and I was in L.A. Jill's apartment was real nice and it was big enough for the two of us. And it was in West Hollywood, on North Alfred Street, only 10 minutes from Ringo's house, just above The Strip there. I could just drive up: Whatever time he needed me, I was there. Simple. It wasn't any formal agreement, it was just, "Oh, okay, I'm here." I moved in with her.

At that time she was working downtown Los Angeles in the garment industry as a designer in an actual design studio. She was trained for that. She went to college in L.A., Parsons College, which is quite well known in the fashion business. She graduated from there, but she was working at the boutique to pay the rent, and then she continued her studies. When she'd finished college she got quite a good job with this big company, Mercedes Nederin I think they were called. She'd commute from West Hollywood to downtown L.A.

West Hollywood was nice, considering it's in the middle of a big city. Lots of good restaurants, better social life. Jill was younger then, so rock 'n' roll and a bit of a drive to work was no problem. In West Hollywood you can walk to a restaurant. Lots of things to do.

So she met Ringo through me, and Keith Moon later on, and various people. People like The Beatles weren't as accessible as just walking into a club and you'd go over to them—unless you really, really knew them. If you didn't you couldn't just stroll up to the table and go, "Hi, I'm Jill." And Jill would never do that anyway. Jill was very discreet.

We used to go to a club called On The Rocks which is above The Roxy. It's like a private club, and nobody knows about it. We'd go up there and see everybody. Lots of movie people went up there as well 'cause it was a seriously private club. People like Ringo and maybe Harry Nilsson, people like Tony Curtis, some of the old lunatic Hollywood people. It was seriously private and you had to be known. But the bouncers and everybody knew me, so I never had any problems. And Jill would come up there with me and we'd have a meal.

It was my idea to get married, absolutely my idea. We'd probably been living together about 9 months, but we'd known each other for a while. So it wasn't just, *bop*, a flash in the pan. I mean, I'd known her for a *long* time, I'd known her since the day I broke her out of her boutique and put the chain on the door. And then at one point it was just…the right time. It was a good time.

On February 11, 1977, Jill and I got married at Ringo's place, on his lawn in Beverly Hills by his pool. Ringo was the best man, and he paid for everything—God bless 'im—the rings, the preacher. The preacher was actress Sally Kirkland, so it was written up in *Variety* magazine.

There were about 15 or 16 people there. It was very, very nice. Donna Summer was at my wedding. A couple of the guys at my wedding, my good friends Mick Coles and Keith Robertson, two English guys who were over here doing their thing, were working for Donna Summer, who was just beginning with the disco rage stuff. She was doing quite well and she was with Casablanca Records, an up-and-coming record company. So anyway Keith and Mick were me mates, so I invited them to the wedding.

They said, "You know, Donna Summer would love to…you know…say hello and meet Ringo and all that. Could we invite her?"

I said, "Yeah, sure." I'd seen her once or twice but I didn't know her. But they were me mates. "Yeah, of course, it'd be good, bring her along." So they brought her to my wedding. She was real cool, and she just stood there with the wedding party, with her boyfriend, said hello to Ringo. She bought me a coupla gifts, and gave everyone a kiss and a hug, and that's how I met Donna Summer. And I knew her people.

Nancy, Ringo's girlfriend, took the photographs. A couple of butterflies came over and flew around my wife's head as we were doing the ceremony, although they didn't show up on the photographs. It was just magical—the big white clouds in the sky, and butterflies over my wife's head. She looked like an angel. And…I cried. I think Ringo had a tear in his eye, 'cause he was fond of me. It was absolutely an honor, a privilege, to have him at my wedding.

Our wedding night we just went back to our little apartment. Ringo loaned me the BMW and some cash and said, "Go to Mexico! Have fun!" We got as far south as Laguna—about and hour, then he called me back. I'd given him numbers, and he found me and called me back. So we didn't have a honeymoon.

Sausage Delivery by Concorde

One particular day while I was living in Monte Carlo with Ringo Starr and his girlfriend Nancy, Ringo went, "Oh, God, I've got all these papers, they've gotta be in New York."

I said, "Oh, okay, fine."

"It's an emergency: They've *gotta* get to New York. I've just signed them. They've gotta be in New York. It's part of this big contract."

"Okay."

"So," he says, "get to London, and then get to New York as soon as you can, because the office has other paperwork for ya too."

"Okay, no problem." That was my job.

I jump a plane to London, get one of the guys to come pick me up and take me to Apple to pick up more paperwork before I find a plane to New York. While I'm at the office waiting for the final envelope for New York, someone says, "Bryan, there's a call for ya."

The phone rings in my little cubbyhole. "Hello?"

"'Allo, Bryan! How's it going?" It was John Lennon, calling from New York.

"Oh, yeah, all right, man! What's the story?"

He says, "Aw, great! I need ya…to get some sausages for me. And get 'em to me as soon as possible." English sausages are a special thing. You just can't get 'em in America. He didn't know I'd just flown in from Monte Carlo with paperwork from Ringo that had to go to New York. I think he just phoned the office 'cause he thought I'd be around.

John says, "I *need* some sausages. Gotta have 'em. I have my account at…."

"Oh, yeah, I know your butcher." Everybody had accounts, had their own private butchers, hairdressers, apple-growers, etc. There were so many accounts, no wonder Apple had so many accountants! It didn't matter what you wanted, you didn't have to pay for it, you just signed for it.

He said, "I've *gotta* have 'em!"

"Well, as it happens, I'm goin' to New York."

"Right! Great! Get up to the butcher shop, get 10 pounds of sausages, stick 'em in your briefcase, and I'll take care of the customs at this end." Never mind the paperwork I've got. And that you're not supposed to be bringin' fresh meat into America.

"Okay…. Yeah."

He said, "Well…, get it! Do it, now!"

"Well, the fastest way is the Concorde."

"Good thinkin'! Do it! Get the Concorde." The Concorde were new at that time, and cost thousands upon thousands of dollars to fly on. John goes, "Just get on the bloody Concorde and get 'ere, now."

It fit in with the paperwork I had to deliver for Ringo, so I said, "Okay!"

I booked the flight, got one of the guys to drive me to get John's sausages, then take me to Heathrow, and jumped on this mach two aeroplane that goes faster than the speed of sound.

You get on this plane and it's just a narrow tube, with 2 seats, an aisle, and 2 seats. That's it. Hmm. The seats are really padded, and they have a shoulder strap! Hmm…okay! That's interesting.

This great plane goes to the end of the runway, revs up like crazy. They let the breaks go, and it just goes like a bullet, zzzzoooooommmmm, down the runway. And then it lifts off, and it goes up at a really sharp angle, like 45 degrees. You're like, "Whoa!" And off it goes.

They want the plane up as high as possible when the sonic boom happens, when it goes through the sound barrier. That's why the plane wasn't so successful in the end—loud. And expensive.

So we're goin' vrrrooooommmmm. There's a big speedometer on the front bulkhead where the flight deck is. And it just rolls off the speed. You're watchin' this thing and it goes dttt-dttt-dttt-dttt-dtt-dtt-dtt, baaaaa. You don't hear the sonic boom 'cause the sound is behind you—physics and all that. You don't even know it happened except the speedometer tells you.

The plane's just going like anything and suddenly I've gone through the sound barrier…with a bag of sausages! This is livin'!

Then it levels off, really high, twice the height of a jumbo jet. The windows are really thick, small, and double-glazed. They get really warm because of the friction. And ever so slightly you think you can see the curvature of the world—that's how high you are.

The stewardesses say, "Champagne?" And it's Moët champagne, the good stuff. "How would you like your steak cooked, Mr. Rooney?"

It's about a 3-hour flight from London to New York. No jet lag. There's just time for a meal, no movies or any of that stuff. You read a magazine and the girls go up and down with the champagne. It was beautiful.

Then the next thing you know, "Fasten your seatbelts, we're coming in for a landing." And you look at your watch and think, "That's impossible," 'cause you're landing before you left—because of the time zone changes. There you are!

I get off the plane about 11 a.m. or so. New York is about 5 or 6 hours behind London so it's daylight. And there's the guy from Allen Klein's management office, a *big* Italian bruiser right out of *The Godfather*. His hands are bigger than my head. In his thick Italian accent he says, "Come with me. C'mon on boy!" and off we go.

No customs. Klein and his Italian people in New York know how to deal with that. Off we go in a bloody big stretch Lincoln or something, straight over to John's place. The limo driver takes the paperwork over to where it's gotta go.

At the Dakota I go up the elevator to John's apartment. John says, "Ah, great! Brilliant! Welcome!" He's happy. "Well done, man! Make me a sandwich."

"Okay." I go in the kitchen and make some sausage sandwiches, which are a Liverpool delicacy. Brilliant.

John and I have the sausage sandwiches, and a gin and tonic or whatever it was. Then I said, "Gotta go!"

He says, "No, no, you can stay the night. What…."

"No, I've got to be back. Ringo needs me and all that."

He says, "Aw, God."

"I'm on a fuel change, you know? The Concorde's fuelin' so I've gotta get back when it's refueled." Same plane, just zap back to London.

So he says, "Oh, okay, never mind. We still coulda gone out and all. Next time!"

"Yeah, sure!"

So I'm back in the limo, bzzzzzzmp, back to Kennedy, back to the Concorde. I'm used to it now, I'm an old hand! "Yes, thank you, I'll have a glass of Moët. And medium rare for my steak."

Zoom, back to London, back to the office. There's a message: "Pick up Ringo at Tramp's."

Ringo's come over to London from Monte Carlo and has gone down to Tramps, which is *the* big club, for *the* people, with great food—they had a French chef, dancin', and rock 'n' roll. There's a little stage where Clapton played, where Jimi Hendrix played "Purple Haze" and all that. It's a great club, but seriously private. You're not allowed in unless you are *known*. Of course they know me because I've spent half me life there.

So even though I just got back from New York, I grab a car and zoom down to Tramp's. Ringo's at a table with a coupla guys, having a drink and just finishing his meal. He goes, "Where've you been?"

"Well, remember that paperwork, I've been in New York. I went to New York this morning, had a word with John, came back tonight, and found your note."

He says, "Oh, right! Well done!" Then, "How'd you…? Where'd…?"

"Took the Concorde."

"Really?"

"Oh, yeah, it was great."

Ringo said, "I've gotta try that. Well done! Good thinkin'! Now, what've you got?"

I said, "I've got the Mercedes Pullman outside."

"Okay, great. Have somethin' to eat, and then you can take me home."

"Okay, cool." I had a nice meal, nice glass of wine, jumped in the car, took him home, then went back to my townhouse at #34 Boston Place, next to Marleybourne Station. And that was just "A Day in the Life" at Apple.

On Tour with Donna Summer

A few months after our wedding, I was getting bored just shuttling Ringo around L.A. to restaurants and parties and things. It was more like being a chauffer. I wanted to do more things. He didn't really have any big projects happening that he could get me excited about. He was doing session work with a coupla guys, but it was nothing interesting for me, you know. I was just running around L.A. in the BMW.

It was sometime in 1977. My mates were still working for Donna Summer, who was with Casablanca. They said, "We need somebody to come and help us with Donna, you interested?" They had some tours coming up for *Once Upon A Time* and said, "We've got things to do, and we need an engineer, a sound engineer, and all that. Are you interested?"

I thought about it for a while. Ringo wasn't doing much, so he wouldn't miss me, really. He was happy, he was just taking it easy, relaxing. He was playing or touring a little with his friends, taking trips, and he had a couple of movie scripts he was reading. So he gave me his blessings, and off I went back into the bloody world of "let's go on the road and do a tour again."

Jill was fine with it. She was very busy with her own career. With me being Donna's sound engineer, Jill knew I'd be out on the road. But even I didn't anticipate we'd be out on tour 6 months at a time. Donna Summer really got hot, and she was in demand everywhere. Her records were really selling, so everybody wanted to go to a concert. So it was, "Okay, off we go," and 6 months later you come back. We took her around the world. We were all over Europe, we were all over South America, North America…we were everywhere with Donna.

It's always tough, yeah, being away from Jill. It's tough. But at the very minimum, 3 times a week I'd talk to her. You get lonely out there. You've finished a gig, you're on your own, had a couple of drinks and you're still on your own, and you're sitting in your room looking through your bloody paperwork for the next gig or whatever's gonna happen, and it's 3 in the morning. I didn't particularly care about the time, I'd call Jill and wake her up.

Stage Manager for Donna Summer

Then I moved up from being Donna's sound engineer to being her assistant stage manager for 1978's *Live and More*, then stage manager for 1979's *Bad Girls*. I designed some of her stages, all the hydraulics. We got *really* big. I had 8, 9 semis full of equipment—a LOT of stuff.

We were using The Who's sound system. They weren't doing anything at that time. The company we used for our production equipment, the sound and lights and all that, was a big English company in Thousand Oaks called Haskell Sound and Lights, a big company owned by a guy called Joe Brown. We always used these guys for our equipment.

After The Who had gone on that particular tour, Joe said, "Listen. We've got a great, brand new sound system. It's The Who's, and they're not using it. Do you wanna lease it?"

Donna was doing *big* stadiums, with a 36-piece orchestra. The Who had a really powerful sound system. It gave you a great mix and a great balance. The German soundboards had 36 channels. So we're like, "Yeah! Yeah, we'll go for that. It'll be perfect." We made a deal, got the sound system down to L.A. and did some rehearsals, and it was brilliant. It was a beautiful sound system.

It also came with a guy called Keith Bradley, who was Eric Clapton's sound engineer, who'd helped put it together. And he wasn't doing anything, so I managed to put him on the payroll for the tour. He's a brilliant sound engineer, absolutely brilliant. He's one of the best in the world, much better than me, and a really good guy. Eric Clapton wouldn't move out of his door without this guy.

And we had a guy called Arnie Thompson on the monitors. Donna was a killer with monitors. She had to have practically more sound on stage than was up front. It was *so loud* on stage it'd make your ears bleed. But that's what she liked. We had side fills; we 6 floor monitors just for her. So, exponentially, the more you gave her, the more the rest of the band needed just to keep up with her, so they could try and hear what *they* were doing.

So it was a huge, *huge* system that we took on the road in the end. But we had a great crew. Mostly English: Eric Clapton's guys, some of my guys, and off we went. These guys weren't doing anything at that time, and they didn't mind going out and earning money. And it sounded killer. With a 36-piece orchestra, you've gotta have some really good sound levels, some good mixing going on.

Our tour manager, Mick Coles, and the promoters, and I, were organizing everything. I was in charge of the equipment. And there's no point in the equipment being there if the crew couldn't be there, so I was in charge of the crew too, and their security and their happiness.

We were doing Mile High Stadium, we were doing the Hollywood Bowl. When we were in America we were doing the major gigs in each city. That's how big she was.

We did soccer stadiums in South America, 60,000 people, sold out. But in South America you had to drive around in armored personnel carriers. There was a lot of drugs, a lot of kidnapping. You'd be scared. It's pretty heavy stuff—kidnapping, terrorism, big, *big* stuff going on down there. And you're trying to entertain these poor people. So you couldn't just travel around in a rent-a-car. We had the army do the transport for us down there, in armored personnel carriers.

I mean, it was crazy down there, especially for our security guys. We'd take over 4 floors of a hotel. Apart from the people staying on 3 floors, 1 floor would just be security. Nobody was allowed past that floor to get near us.

How I Lost My Front Teeth

We were doing a whole European thing and then we were going down to Italy, which was disco crazed. Everyone was dancing. It was total madness down in Italy—they're very passionate people.

We were playing in new discotheques, I'm talking about 7,000 people capacity. They were huge. They were built in the middle of farm fields, outside of towns. They'd have hydraulic stages that came up and out, and you could take apart the dance floor with hydraulics and that would be your stage. They had their own sound systems, their own light systems. So they're kind of easy to do in terms of sound and lights 'cause they'd have very good equipment, a lot of German equipment. A lot of the tour was that.

We'd also be doing opera houses.... You'd pull into the town, and you'd find again it's an opera house. Of course, these venues were not built for our equipment. The stage is 3 floors up. You had to take stuff up to the stage outside, with a block-and-tackle, up through windows you'd taken the frames out of, just to get it up to the stage. And then reverse to get it back down to your truck and haul away. Opera houses weren't built to accommodate tons of rock 'n' roll equipment, they were built for a guy to carry his instrument up the stairs. And opera singers, you don't need to carry them, they just walk. But *we* had to move all this stuff, and it was chaos! But we did it.

At one particular place, a sports arena in Milan, we'd set up, and we were doing sound checks and everything. I think there were about 12,000 people waiting outside. And there's a whole ruckus outside the doors because we hadn't let anybody in yet. There's smashing and bashing and crashing and everything. But it went away.

Then they let the people in, and you could tell there's tension in the air. There's people pushing and shoving and stuff.

We get on stage, and Donna starts. We get into about the 2nd number and a whole bunch of fighting breaks out. People are throwing things, and one of our Italian bodyguards is saying that these people want their money back, that it's "free music!" and they're not going to pay. It was like a bunch of Red Brigade terrorists. Well, I don't know who they were. But they were drinking, and they were throwing things at the stage.

We took Donna off because it was too dangerous…and they stormed the stage! They were just tearing it down! Somebody set fire to one of the PA rings, and it went up in bloody smoke…I mean, *thousands* of dollars worth of equipment was just going up in flames.

Well, the Italian police just disappeared. As per the usual M.O., they didn't want to get involved. Me and my crew and a couple of our lads and our security guys are alone stage among the rioters because I didn't want to lose everything! Otherwise the whole tour…. God. What are you gonna do? We'd have to buy everything again. Is the insurance gonna cover it? The whole tour would be screwed and the next town in line, and the next town, and *everybody* loses money.

So we were in a big battle on stage. One of the bloody clowns gets hold of one of our mike stands and swings it at me. I didn't see it coming.

Hits me in the face. And my front teeth just go ka-dunk. There was blood pouring out me. I thought he'd broke me nose, but it was my teeth. I spotted the bastard who did it, and we were battling back and forward. The police finally came back and pulled their clubs and stuff, and managed to fight the stage clear.

But the one guy who'd got me had run backstage, and I caught up with him with a couple of my guys. And I was, well, *seriously annoyed* with this guy, which was apparent. I was in no mood for any kind of chat.

So I grabbed him. And so did one of my guys, Phil DeMonte, I think it was, my keyboard guy. He's great. He's from Liverpool as well. He and I grabbed this bastard, and I put him over two flight cases. And I picked up a stage weight and dropped it on him and broke one of his legs. Then I broke one of his arms over the flight case. He was seriously screaming. He was seriously not a happy Italian. But that's what you get if you start it, you know. I was *not* a happy camper. So I broke a coupla limbs for him and kicked him in the face a few times too just for the fun of it.

After that there was no point going to hospital. My teeth were gone. What're you gonna do? There's nothing a hospital can do. I had a bottle of cognac and a coupla pain killers. We had a tour doctor—we always had a doctor on tour with us who would give us painkillers and things. It was always handy to have a doctor on the road. He was an American guy, just come out of internship. He was real nice, a professional. He put a coupla stitches in my lip, and a couple on my nose.

As for how Jill felt about me having no front teeth, I guess she didn't care. I was already missing one of them when I met her, so the gap just got wider. I mean, I'm not exactly the best looking guy on the planet, you know! She just thought I was cute, I guess.

And I left the teeth missing like this. I look like a pirate! It can help you 'cause it can be intimidating. You know, if you're doing a show in New York and you're shouting and screaming at a bunch of Local 1 Union Teamsters at Madison Square Garden, and you're trying to get your way, and they don't want to do it *your* way, they have to do it *their* way, then you can stand up and shout and scream and swear—and you got no teeth and you don't mind spitting—you might be able to get a few points out of it. You might be able to intimidate somebody to do something that they didn't wanna do, even though they were supposed to do it.

And I'm not vain. If people don't like it, well, look the other way, or don't talk to me. I suppose that's arrogant. But at the same time it's not. And look at me: Aren't I lovely? I'm…whatever. Bollocks! I'm a dirty, scruffy bastard from Liverpool anyway.

Anyway, we'd hustled Donna out. The promoter had a white Rolls Royce, of all things, that we were using for Donna. We threw her in the back with her security people. We had Bear, big Bear from The Rainbow, and we had Muhammad Ali's security guy, James Anderson. Muhammad Ali lived just around the corner from Donna, in Hancock Park in L.A. So James Anderson was the bodyguard for the best fighter in the world. Big, *big* black guy, James. Very elegant: Silk Italian suits, always had a tie on, licensed to carry guns and all that. A very, very together guy. He's done a lot of good stuff. And Muhammad Ali at that point wasn't doing much of anything, so Donna approached James and he became our head of security. Lovely man.

So James was in the Rolls with Donna, and they just got the hell out of there, "Bollocks! Go!" Get her back to the hotel and just leave her alone. We didn't need her anywhere near us when all this was going down. You don't want to be worrying about her when you're worrying about a million bucks worth of her equipment. You don't need a superstar hiding down in the bloody dressing room waiting for the place to burn down. So you get 'em out as quick as you possibly can.

Donna thanked us, and we got a bonus. For almost dying. But no, it was fine.

Billionaire's Party—and Jail

Casablanca Records in L.A. got a phone call: A guy wants Donna to do his wife's birthday party. The call was actually from the French guy in charge of the entertainment at the *Folies Bergère* in Paris, the big club with the world famous can-can dancers and all that stuff. He's putting this gig together for this German billionaire, and he wants Donna to come and play at this guy's house in a place called Klagenfurt in Austria.

So, of course, Donna's manager goes, "We're not going to do a private party. We can do a 50,000-seat stadium. We can't do a private party …what do you think this is?"

It turns out the guy is willing to pay 2 million dollars! Or something like that. The number was outrageous. So…nobody's stupid enough to turn that down…and if it's an easy gig anyway, you think…. You *think*.

Our agent from William Morris gets hold of me and Mick and says, "Right, we're doing a gig…. What's the minimum you can take with you? We'll rent as much as possible where we're going."

I says, "Where are we going?"

"Well, we're going to this guy's estate in Austria. And we're gonna play, I don't know, in some room in his house."

"Okay…. We need the band, obviously, and the girls, the backup vocalists." There was a 9-piece rhythm section, and I said, "I can fly their equipment from here, and over there they have to supply us with a coupla stand lights, and a small PA. If it's only gonna be in a room in the house," I said, "there's no point in getting stupid about it, right?"

We get that part settled and he says, "Okay. Here's the plan. The guy's gonna fly *everybody* first class from L.A. to Paris. Everybody—the crew, the band, everybody. And then, the guy owns his own Boeing 707 jet." What was his name? Baron something. He owned one of the biggest pharmacy companies in Europe. The guy's a billionaire. "We're gonna fly to Paris, get on his private jet, fly down to Austria, then drive over to his house. He's in a town called Klagenfurt."

"Okay, sounds good. No problem."

So we all get it organized, get the equipment, put it on the same jet we're gonna fly. We get to Paris and transfer everything to this guy's private commercial jet. It really is a 707. And there's all sorts of people getting on board, all these weird people: a band of gypsies, Greek people, belly dancers, jugglers….

What we didn't realize is that the guy who runs the *Folies Bergère* in Paris has put together a whole smorgasbord of the best people in the world that this guy wanted for his wife's birthday. So they're the best belly dancers from Turkey, jugglers from China, an opera singer, all of Donna Summer's rabble, a mariachi band…! We get it all together in Paris, and then we all get on this private 707 jet.

I said, "Nobody told me…!"

"Ah, don't worry, it's okay," says the guy who's putting it together, this French dude. He's a real cool guy. And off we go…okay! No problem.

We get all the gear and all the people to a hotel in Klagenfurt. The guy's taken over the whole hotel for all the performers.

We go up to his estate to check it out the day before. His estate is …mega. This guy's security guys are in their own uniforms, with Dobermans and Alsatians everywhere. Helicopters, guns…you know, the usual billionaire stuff.

I said, "Nice. Okay, where's the gig?"

They take us into the house. He had different stages in different rooms around the house for the different gigs by different people. We're in the guy's bowling alley—his own bowling alley, right? They put this little stage where the pins are. The PA system's pretty much a domestic system, for a home, with a bunch of cabinets stacked every which way.

I groaned. I said, "Oh…, okay, so this is…. Well…. Okay, I've got it." I get all the band gear on the stage, and then I said, "Look, guys, nobody gets miked up. Only Donna and the 3 girls get mikes. The rest of you: No turning up. Everything's gotta be set the way I want it. And it's gonna be number 4 for everybody on your amps. And you, the drummer, and the bloody percussionist, keep it down. 'Cause there's nowhere for the sound to go."

"Okay, yeah yeah," they say.

The day of the party there's at least 250 people in tuxedos. The dressing room area for Donna and all the different people was down in the pool house. It was an Olympic size pool indoors, 'cause it gets cold over there. The guy owns a yacht on the Mediterranean, it's like the Onassis Yacht, and he's got a radar-controlled perfect model of it in the swimming pool. We…turned it on…and crashed it. Nobody cared; I mean, the guy's a billionaire.

He's got a miniature radio-controlled helicopter, which one of our guys was quite good at. We were flying it around the swimming pool area, chk-chk-chk…. That crashed somewhere down the line as well.

It's getting time for us to go on. They've got a sword eater before us, and some guy juggling flames and stuff. What the hell?

I noticed before we went on that it was like *The Gong Show*. If he didn't like somebody who was performing for him, he'd just put up his hand, and this promoter guy would go over to the performer and go, "Ahem. Next!" And you're off!

Oh, God, he won't…. What happens if he just tells Donna to go! There's gonna be *chaos*! She'll go berserk…she'll kick him!

When it was our turn to go on, I get the band on, make sure everything's cool, and then we get Donna on.

He loves Donna. The guy was like 80 and his wife was like 35 years old, you know, the usual. But he loved Donna, loved her dress and everything, "More! More!" So we have to do an encore for him.

When we finished that, I got all our gear off and into a little van that they'd rented us, and that was to go back to the airport 2 days later. We were gonna spend a coupla days at this guy's expense in this little town called Klagenfurt. It was a beautiful little place. The hotel was great, and there were a coupla clubs in town.

So we're out of the gig in half an hour 'cause we didn't have much stuff. Get in one of the limos, down to the hotel, get changed, and me and the lighting director say, "Let's go out to a club, have a few drinks." We've got these passes from the billionaire that basically gives us access to anything, 'cause he owns the town.

We get into this really nice, private club, got a table and everything. Coupla girls around, people dancing and stuff. "Okay, fine, yeah, that's cool."

I said to the waitress, "Gin and tonic. And he's gonna have a scotch and Coke." She brings bottles. You don't just get a drink in a glass, they bring you the glass and ice, and they bring you a full bottle. Stupid! But, well, okay.

We make our drinks, do a bird dance, mess about a bit, then, "Let's go somewhere else."

They bring us the bill, and it's like, "WHAT?" Whatever the currency was, we translated it into dollars and it was like 500 bucks! For 2 bottles of booze. So me mate was *not* amused, and said, "I'm not paying that! Do you think I'm stupid? I can go down to the local drugstore and buy a bottle for 10 bucks. What're you talking about?"

We got into it. They got some bouncers over, and we were our own bouncers, so we started a fight. They called the police or constables, who come steaming into the club, and we get arrested. So we didn't pay the bill. We just got dragged out and thrown into the cop cars.

The cops have got us in the bloody cars, and they've got an inspector who speaks English. I'm explaining to him the injustice of the whole deal, and how these bouncer guys tried to pick us up off the floor.

And then he notices the guy's name on this card I've got, and he's like, "You're….!"

"We've just been at the bloody…."

He's like, "Oh, no, this is bad news…for everyone." It's not very cool to be arresting one of the entertainers for this guy who owns the town.

They take us down to the jailhouse, and he's like, "Okay, now, let me sort it out. Look," he points to us, "you go in that room. You go in that room. And I'll make some phone calls and we'll get it figured out."

Oh, we were really peppy, "Oh, okay, yeah, sure."

So we each go in our rooms and *clang*! It's a trick. It's a cell! I'd thought it was going to be an interview room or something. *Clang, click*!

"Ah, man!"

"Bastard!" We were screaming at him.

Then I looked around. Really nice bed. *Really* nice bed! Feather pillows, tartan Scottish wool blankets, my own little bathroom. This is a cell? And me mate's next door. I go, "Hey, how are you?"

He says, "Aw, I'm fine, I'm all right. It's better than the bloody hotel, this."

I said, "All right. I'll see you in the morning!" We'd had the bottles to drink, remember. So we just fell asleep.

The next morning, knock knock—they *knock* on the cell door. A cop opens the door, and he's got a tray with croissants and coffee and fruit. Room service! "Have your breakfast, and we've got a couple of questions, huh?"

"No problem."

So we eat breakfast, then the inspector's like, "Okay…, look. Look, the bill was a bit much, I understand that. But, um, you were, you did drink it."

I said, "Oh, no problem. Yeah, we drank it and all that and we just got a bit out of order, and I apologize. And tell the bouncers I'm sorry and everything. Give me the bill, I'll go back to my hotel and take care of it."

He says, "Well, it's been taken care of. They paid the bill. They didn't want any trouble."

"Oh…. Okay."

"Everything's cool. Come on, I'll give you a ride back to the hotel."

We get back in another police car, and they drive us back to our hotel. Like a lot of European hotels, this one has a patio on the street where they serve breakfast.

The car pulls up outside the hotel right by the breakfast area. Me and me mate, well, we're hung over. We stagger out the bloody cop car.

And there's Donna. And the manager. And the promoter from bloody France. And some of the band. And a coupla our guys, the crew. They're all sitting on the patio having breakfast.

We're laughing. "Morning!"

Donna looks at us like, "Oh, no, now what?" She said, "What've you been doing?"

I said, "Oh…, we got lost in town, and the guys just brought us home."

She said, "Oh, that's nice."

I said, "Yes, nice. I'll have a coffee, and some meat and eggs, please."

So yeah, we got busted…but we got away with it.

Donna Summer's Adventure on Her Crew's Plane

Donna had a Lear Jet. Because the gigs were so crazed, and thanks to the agent, and the promoter Alan Tinkley (I think), God bless him, I had to get a plane for my crew too. We had 2 systems, the A and B systems, that would leapfrog because of the distances between gigs. So it's really not just 8 semis, more like 16 semis of equipment leapfrogging each other, each one a duplicate of the next one.

So me and the crew had a DC-3 prop plane. Ah, God! Donna and her secretaries, and her hangers-on, and her boyfriend, and the security people, had a 16-seater, a Gulfstream or a Lear. They were in that, and we had a DC-3, HAHA!

So it would always be that all the crew were like, "*Yeah*! Finished the gig!" then would pack the trucks, get to the airport, and we'd all bail in for the flight to the next town. People are smoking pot. Doing coke. Pills. Everyone has a different sound system, like Walkmans.

And the pilots are like, "Yeah!" They were great: 2 ex-Vietnam guys, brilliant men. These guys have got on leather helmets, with the ear flaps. Off we go!

We could barely take off, 'cause we had so much shit in the belly of the plane. The luggage compartment also carried a lot of our tools. And we had a lot of Donna's costume…stuff…in the belly of the plane. And all of our suitcases. We'd be skimming trees before they got the wheels up. We could only fly at about 400 feet. You could open the windows. There was no pressurization, you'd just open the windows, throw cigarettes and shit out. It was brilliant.

On one particular tour we'd done about 5 gigs with the plane. I'm at the hotel one night, and knock-knock, "Yeah, right, up to Donna's suite. Now."

Oh, God, what's she want? It's gotta be serious. Put on a clean T-shirt, sprayed myself with some aftershave or something, then up to the top floor. Donna's got the whole floor booked for herself and her entourage. Her suite has a doorbell. Ding-dong at the door.

I go, "I'm shattered. What's the problem?"

Her guy says, "Come in."

I said, "Gimme a drink." She's got a bar in her suite. "What's the plan? What's the problem?"

"I hear you guys are having a *lot* of fun on your airplane."

I went, "Oh…yeah…. Who told you that?"

It was Barry the Bag. Barry the Bag was related to one of The Brooklyn Dreams, our opening act. Donna was going out with one of The Brooklyn Dreams, Bruce Sudano, and she's now married to him. The Brooklyn Dreams was 3 guys, and they used our equipment and our band as a backup, so we didn't have to shump bands back and forth. It was 3 guys, 3 mikes. Nice guys.

One of their cousins or brothers-in-law, Barry, needed a job. I was told to give him a job on the crew. This guy is a big oaf. No brains.

"What's a amp?" Hasn't got a clue. And I've gotta find this guy a gig, because of Donna, and she's gonna pay him.

I says "All right. Fine. I'm gonna put him in charge of the baggage." We're traveling with about 30 people. That's a lot of luggage. I said, "Look, right. We're on the gig, he's the bag boy." So we called him Barry the Bag. His gig was to get all the luggage off the areoplanes.

And he was like, "I work for Donna Summer."

I said, "See all these bags? You've gotta get 'em from here to the hotel, and every bag delivered to every room, every day. That's your job. Right?" We were paying him $500 bucks a week or something. Hell of a lot of money! "It's really easy, right? I've color-coded everything. Everybody'll have their own number. You'll have a master sheet. Every time we go to a hotel, you get the list of everybody's room, transpose it to your master sheet, and deliver all the bags. I'll give you X amount of money a week for tips for the bell boys. Just get everybody's bags to their room. Every morning the bags will be outside their doors. Get 'em back with the bell boys, back to the vans to take the shit to the airport. All right?"

"Got it."

Not hard. So he was flying with us, the crew, not Donna, 'cause he's part of the crew. And now he'd grassed me up to his brother-in-law or whatever he was, Bruce Sudano from The Brooklyn Dreams, about what was going on on our areoplane. About the pot and the coke and the heroin and the music and the dancing girls, about the stewardesses in their miniskirts.

I had said to the stewardesses, "You know, the best thing you could do is to sit in the back, right? Leave the drink carts out front, and don't worry about it. Just enjoy yourself. Join the party." Nice girls actually. Some of the guys called them every now and again.

So all this is going on on our plane. You open the door, and a whole bunch of smoke just wafted out at the airport, right? It was chaos.

So anyway, I'm in the meeting with Donna, and she goes, "I wanna fly on your airplane."

"I need another drink." Then I said, "Donna, you *don't* wanna come near our aeroplane. Your voice is worth a million bucks, right? Our areoplane is a...den of iniquity. You don't wanna be on it."

"Nope, I'm bored on my..., what is it?"

I said, "It's a million-dollar aeroplane! It's a jet, it gets you from A to B, zoom! We're clippin' trees. I could put me hand out the window and grab a pigeon! You *don't* wanna be on our areo—! It's the *crew* plane!" I went on, "Half the time it's the only chance we get to relax, because, seriously, we land, and we're off to the next gig to pick up the A unit or the B unit. All 8 semis! It's the only chance we get to have a break, and then we go to our hotels, and die."

She said, "No, that's it. I'm paying, it's my money, I'm comin' on your airplane."

"When?"

"Tonight."

"You're not gonna be happy...." Then I thought, well, fuck it! I ain't gonna do nothing. Bollocks!

So we finish the gig and get in the limousines and zoom out to airport. Donna gets on. And her personal secretary Pat Naderhoff, who just died recently, actually. God bless her. I went down to her funeral a few months ago. God, that was a heavy one....

Anyway, Donna, Pat, and James her bodyguard, and a couple of her yes-people, the brownnosers, come over to our DC-3.

We get on the plane—our plane—and Donna's up front.

The pilots are used to having a joint before they take off, right? One of our techs would just roll 'em a couple of joints and throw 'em in, "Here, lads!" There would be the sound of inhaling then, "Okay, we're ready!" You'd hear the propellers, then bang bang, steam, fuel, bang, off we go. We're hurtling down the runway.

Donna was sucking in air, in fear.

I'm thinking, "Welcome to the real world." I'm way back in the back by the bathrooms—I'm sensible.

And everyone goes, "Bryan?" They know I've got 12 skinners of good hash from England. And grass. I go, "Yeah! Here we go, lads!"

They didn't care Donna was on board. She was just the singer. We're chopping out lines, snort. And there's music everywhere.

It was, "Hey, you fucked up on that lighting cue," etc. We're just talking about the gig. Bollocks! A crew's life is a crew's life, you know. You have a good crew like that, most of them are English, and they're all arrogant. They only cared about *their* gig. They do their gig, and it'd better be nice on stage, and look great, and sound great, and then everyone's happy. They don't give a monkey's wedding about what that…spot…on the stage thinks. That's just the wage-payer, right? Just a little ant. Who cares what Donna Summer says?

I know what I'm doing, and these guys are pulling *huge* cables all day. They don't care who is on the plane or not. And I wasn't gonna say, "Aw, listen, guys, cool it." 'Cause they'd certainly throw me out the window. They would have!

So, again, the plane is just a fog of marijuana smoke, cocaine bursts, and God knows what else. There's booze. And…yo! The stewardesses have got their skirts up high! It was just like a bunch of Vikings.

We land, bang bang, I think in Atlanta, bang bang bang bang bang, crash, bang, land. Open the door and a *big* plume of smoke blows out the aeroplane.

Donna and her crowd get off and there's a couple a limos waiting. The rest of us fall down the stairs and open up the belly of the plane to get our suitcases. "Hey, Barry the Bag! Where's the…? Get my suitcases in that van." Then we get into our vans and all hail over to hotel. "Right, carry on."

Sure as you know, next morning I'm at the gig at 5 a.m. By this time I'm Production Manager: First man in, last man out. Gotta get the lights up, then the stage, the hydraulics. Big gig. So I'm all shattered when we finish the gig.

And we've got a day off! I remember it clearly. But then knock-knock, "Right! Up to Donna's suite."

It's like going to the headmaster at school. I didn't even bother with a new T-shirt. I was shagged out. Wasted.

I get in the elevator, rrrrrrr, down the corridor. James is outside, the security guy. "Not again," I said. What's happening, man?"

He said, "Oh, she's not happy."

I said, "I don't give a fuck."

"Oh, you're in trouble, Bryan...."

"Thanks for the warning, man." Knock-knock.

"Sit down." Donna, her boyfriend, and Susan Munao the manager are there. I didn't even ask, I just went straight to the bar, poured myself a huge gin and tonic. Lit a cigarette.

Donna fakes coughing and says, "No smoking!"

"Stand outside. I'll smoke it. What's the story?"

Donna goes, "Well, that was an interesting flight last night."

Oh good, she's gonna crack. I said, "Well, you know, I *told* you, I *warned* ya. You know, you've got a Gulfstream billion-dollar jet there, and you wanna fly with this bunch of Viking drunken crazed fools, and you insisted," I said. "Yep, you're paying, you can do whatever you want."

She said, "Right! I want a 'No Smoking' section."

"Oh, come on, Donna, you've gotta be joking!"

"Nope! I love it, I loved the fun. But my throat's hurting."

I said, "I'm not surprised!" Probably a pound of weed got smoked in the 4 hours or whatever we were aloft. I'm truly not surprised.

She said, "That's it. I'm gonna fly on that plane again, and I want a 'No Smoking' section."

I said, "Let me think about this."

"And remember, I'm paying!"

And her manager, Susan Munao, goes, "That's right, and I'm coming on the flight this time."

Oh, this is getting fucking worse! What am I gonna do now? I says, "Right I'll work it out, don't worry." But I'm thinking, "Fuck you!" Bastards.

So I go downstairs and call a meeting with the crew, in the bar. "Right. I want everybody in the fucking bar. The drinks are on Donna."

Chris the lighting director and all the techs turn up, and the schleppers, and the guys in charge of the stage. Everybody.

I said, "Right. Anything you want tonight is on Donna Summer. Just keep drinking. We've got a problem."

"What's the problem, man?"

"Donna wants to keep flying with us. She thinks it's so much fun."

And everyone goes, "WHAT? But we tried to make it really horrible!"

I said, "You didn't!"

They said, "Well, we thought we could help you out there, man."

"You bastards!"

"No, we really tried to be obnoxious, you know, to kick her off the fucking airplane."

"Well, she had such a great time, she wants a 'No Smoking' section."

They're all, "Aw, *no!*"

"So we've gotta figure it out."

I think. Then I said, "I know! We've got rolls of Visqueen." Visqueen is heavy duty clear plastic sheeting that we used to seal off part of the backstage area. It's like drop cloths for painting, really thick and heavy. Anyway, I said, "Right. We've got rolls of Visqueen in one of the fuckin' trucks?"

They said, "Right, yeah, we've got that."

"Right. We've got staple guns?"

"Yep."

"Okay, then, what we need: You: Off to the fuckin' trucks." I sent a couple of lads down to one of the trucks backstage, 'cause the trucks were still at the gig. "Get a couple of rolls of Visqueen, get some of those power staples, a hell of a long length of power cord, and a generator. Oh, and some Velcro. Male and female Velcro. The big stuff, the wide stuff."

"Oh, okay, Bryan, well done."

I said, "Off you go, see ya, come back when you've got it all together."

Then I said, "Here's the plan, guys. Right. We'll get a 'No Smoking' section, right? Easy piece of piss, really, if you think about it."

We get all the gear, get a couple a limos, scoot down to the airport, find the plane. It wasn't even locked. The stairs were still down. The pilots were still drunk somewhere else.

I've got a couple of my guys, and we all bail on the plane.

I said, "Right, we've got...1, 2, 3, 4...6 seats for Donna and her rabble. Oh, 9 seats, we'll go back another row. Right. We'll cut the Visqueen up the middle, and overlap it, right? Glue Velcro on it, and then just staple-gun it all way around the aeroplane, into the beams." Ge-dunk, ge-dunk. Bastards!

We tape it to the floor and we make a flap doorway between the front and back. For the front it was okay 'cause all the smoke was going to be in the back, and as I said, you can open the windows 'cause you're only flying at 400 feet.

We do the gig, then the next night, we go to the airport. Right, here we go!

As everyone gets on the plane they look around and they're seriously like, "Bryan...! What a giggle!" So they've got more pot than usual, and they've got more coke than usual, and they got more booze than usual, and a couple of girls they'd managed to find who didn't mind going to the next gig, wherever it was. And the stewardesses.

The pilots get on, and we give 'em a couple a joints, and I said, "Look. We have a 'No Smoking' section. Don't let her see you smoking." I put some Velcro on the pilots' curtain, behind them. There wasn't a door, just a curtain so they could close off their bit. And we'd taped off the plastic around our section.

Donna and her rabble get on board, and we're all in the back going, "Hee hee hee."

Donna sits down, "Hmm." Then she goes, "What's *that*? Get Bryan here!"

So I open the Velcro flap, walk into the front. I said, "You're in the 'No Smoking' section! Look, it's sealed. So, you know, the boys can do their thing, you can sit in here, in peace, with no smoke bothering your throat, with your people. We're in the back. We'll see you at Chicago" or wherever the hell we were going.

Donna's like, "You're very clever, aren't you."

I said, "No, I'm not.... I'm just trying to help. It's your money, remember? Just trying to help. It's your money."

She's tapping her fingernails.

We take off, and everyone's like, "Yay! Bryan! Rock 'n' roll! Jimmy Hendrix! Yay! Party." And whatever was happenin', was happenin'. We're grooving along. And it worked because we had opened our sliding windows and the smoke blew out.

Got to the other end. Bang, bang, landed. Donna gets off, the rest get off.

Donna gets into her limo, and I go running down the plane's steps, knock on her window, zzzzzzp, "Okay, Donna! How was that? Smoke-free environment. Isn't it lovely? How's your throat?"

She goes, "I think I'll go back to my plane. It's not the same, is it?"

"Well, you know, there's only one way I could do it. I *can't* tell my guys they can't...."

She said, "Ah, you're right. Okay."

I think we did 3 flights with her. She did 1 more, and then she got bored with it. She couldn't actually shout at me, "I'm payin' for this!" Because it was, "I *know* you're payin' for it."

So I got away with it and she left me alone about flying with us. We tore down that smoking section because the pilots were pissed off 'cause they weren't getting all the aftereffects. Without it, they could just open their curtain, inhale, "Ah, lovely," and keep on flying. It was great.

At the end everyone was going, "Well done, Bryan. Got rid of her."

Meeting El Presidente in Santo Domingo

We were down in the Caribbean doing Puerto Rico, Venezuela, and the islands off Venezuela. The Santo Domingo gig was insane. Santo Domingo is the capital of what was then a little dictatorship off in the Caribbean, Dominican Republic, led by El Presidente Joaquin Balaguer.

They told us we were going and we were like, "What the hell is down there?" But then we said, "Okay," because they're paying for us to come play there.

So me and Chris the lighting director flew in to Puerto Rico for the first gig on that leg. Puerto Rico is like part of America, so the equipment, the sound system, the lighting system, were…they weren't the best in the world, but they were close enough. We could do the gig, get away with it. Shine it on, as it were.

So from there Chris and I fly on a little puddle jumper aeroplane over to Santo Domingo. The gig's in a hotel, not a huge stadium like we're used to. But they're paying, and they're paying a fortune. And for them it really had nothing to do with ticket prices, it's all to do with ego: "Donna Summer is coming to our hotel." I mean, you'd have to charge 5,000 bucks a person to break even. So the hotel was picking up the bill, just to say "Oh, we've got Donna Summer." It's like nowadays, what's her bloody name? Paris Hilton. She charges like $20,000 to appear at a club for 40 minutes, just to sit there and drink and have a dance. And that's it, then she's like, "I'm out of here." That's how Paris Hilton earns her money.

So anyway, this gig in a hotel was a prestige thing. Now, the president of Santo Domingo's going to be there with his girlfriend-slash-wife, and all these…slave owners, and God knows who, mafia maybe. Santo Domingo was seriously third world then.

So we get there, get the promoter, and go over to the hotel where the room is where we're playing. They've just got a couple of little speakers, 1 or 2 lights. The stage is no bigger than a backyard swimming pool.

I said, "Oh, yeah…. Um, alright, now, remember the contract we sent ya? You know, it was like 20 pages of technical information and requirements? It's gotta be done. Otherwise, we have every right just to turn 'round and fly out."

The guy's freaking, going, "*Oh, no no*! It's okay. We've got the equipment. Now you have to come down and approve it."

"Oh, okay. That sounds reasonable."

So we get in his Mercedes and go into downtown Santo Domingo, to Santo Domingo Norte.

I mean, I've seen slums, and I've seen barrios, and I've seen bad places. This place took the biscuit. It was just…. There's people dyin' in the streets! There's dead people! There's dead donkeys! There's just death!

It *stinks*. And there's people carrying shit on their heads, and there's people fallin' over. I was in shock.

We pull up to this furniture store. A *furniture* store, right?

"We're here."

I go to get out, and he goes, "DON'T MOVE!"

He's got 2 of his bodyguards with us, and they jump out, and pull the guns, right? And they've got submachine guns, like Uzis. They're scanning the street, and I'm looking at me mate like, "All right.... Could be a bit of trouble here, you know that."

Then the one guy knocks on the door of this furniture store, bang-bang. You hear a crash-bang inside. This little old guy comes and opens the door, and they grab us out the back of the Mercedes and just throw us through the doorway into the store! It wasn't like, "Here, thank you." They just picked us up and threw us. Because they don't want us to be slaughtered, apparently. Brilliant. But I wasn't nervous, just trying to figure out what's happening.

All right. So we're in this place, and there's just furniture. And there's rats running around, in and out the furniture. Okay.... We're cool. "Where's the sound system?"

"Ah-ah, mm-mm, no prob, *no problemo*!"

Down the back of the store, the guy opens a padlock, opens this bloody big door, and we go in. There's a warehouse, and it's *full*. This is the sound system, right? The warehouse is *full* of Tannoy shit. And it's all painted gray. There are great big amplifiers, with 1 switch: on/off. And horns...off battleships! It's scrap U.S. Navy crap. "All hands on deck! All hands on deck!" Ahhhh!

The guy's got a big smile, and pulls down a bottle of goddamn local rum, "Ya da! *Riva, riva*! Sound system! *Si*?" Like, "We're clever."

It's got microphones from the '40s, about 6 inches tall, on a stand.

I go, "Oh, I can't believe it." I said, "No, no.... This is...this is *not* a sound system, this is off a bloody aircraft carrier. You can't, I *can't* put a band, an orchestra, Donna Summer, and 3 singers in front of *that*!" It's just gonna sound like Minnie Mouse or something. It's not gonna sound like anything. "It doesn't work like that."

He says, "Oh, no, it's great!" And he hits this guy over the head to make him turn something on, and he picks up a microphone. He's like, "HELLO!" and we hear "HELLO-LO-LO-LO-LO-LO-LO!"

I said, "Look, see? Look, it's got echo." I said, "No, no, no."

The guy's getting really agitated with us. But we've got 3 days before the gig. What are we gonna do here? I said, "Back to the hotel. Now. Quick. Everybody."

I don't know what language they were speaking, Portuguese or something, I haven't got a clue. But I said, "Back to the hotel, let's go."

And he's like, "Oh, *no*, it's, these are…."

I said, "No. Not usin' it. It's…it's stupid. It's just not gonna happen. I can't put that in a hotel room, in a bloody ballroom, you know, it's just doesn't work like that."

"Aw, no!"

"Stop. Let's get back to the hotel. Come on."

We get back to the hotel, and they've given us suites overlooking the ocean. Bit funky, but really nice. But you know you're in trouble, 'cause it was just like in Venezuela: They have the bed legs in bowls of water so the insects just drop in the bowl of water, so they don't crawl into your bed. And you've got mosquito nets with holes in them. There's all sorts of shit crawling around. So you know you're in trouble anyway. You just know. Plus Santo Domingo is humid. It's like a sauna.

What are we gonna do? All right, all right. Look, we were just…, I know. Got it. Got the plan. We were just in Puerto Rico, and they've got a sound system in Puerto Rico.

So I go back through my tour book, find the sound company in Puerto Rico, and I call 'em. I said, "Right. Look, I'm in Santo Domingo."

"How are ya? Oh, yeah, great! Great, man."

I said, "Listen, I'm in Santo Domingo and I need your sound system. Is it available?"

"Uh…yeah. No problem."

"Right. Put it on a goddamn aeroplane, you and 3 of your techs, *now*. I don't mean tomorrow, I mean *now*. Charter an aeroplane, and we'll bill it to the president." I don't care. I'm bold now. I'm determined to do the gig, right, 'cause it's such a challenge.

I said, "Just charter a DC-3, anything that flies, put your sound system on it, get it here. Okay? Your landing rights? Okay, anything you want. Send the bill to the promotion company here." The guy who's promoting is the president's nephew or something anyway, right? And the place in Puerto Rico didn't give a monkey's wedding. I said, "Oh, and while you're at it, send some lights over, we're gonna need that, and some power distribution, cables, all the stuff you're gonna need. Fill an aeroplane with equipment. 'Cause this goddamn island ain't got nothing but rats and dead people."

The guy's laughing. He said "I've never been...."

I said, "You live on the next island over. What do you mean you've never been here?"

"Well, we avoid it."

"Well, now you're doin' it. 'Cause it's Donna Summer."

"Yeah, I know."

"All right. Get your gear over here, pal."

So sure enough, he flew in a system and some lights and stuff. And we got it together. I put them on stage, and it came out quite good that night.

So after the first night, of course, my nerves are wracked. I'm shattered. At the soundboard, I'm like, "Oh, God," wondering if the power's gonna hold up, 'cause the lights are flickering.

But we got through the first night, so we're gonna be all right. We're down in the casino afterward. There's gambling over there. There's no rules, there's no laws, it's just whatever's going on. And it's like the movie *Casablanca*: Ver-y sha-dy people. Ver-y dodgy. Everyone's got a bulge—a weapon, and white dinner jackets and twisters (bowties). But the dinner jackets are frayed. They're all pretending to be what they're not, "Oh, we're in the casino." There were some really…raggedy-ass…women. They've got pearls on, but the high heels are broke. But this is high society in Santo Domingo, right?

So we're in the casino, and we're pissing about and drinking, and… mainly drinking. There's this little guy who looks like Napoleon, and he's like, "Ah! *Riva!*" He's clapping toward us, and he's sending us drinks and everything.

I go, "Oh, great. Nice to see ya, pal. Well done." Me and Mick and Chris the lighting director are just talking.

Then this little guy comes over and starts interrupting us. Chris goes, "Go away," or something. Chris got really pissed off. He didn't want to talk to the guy.

Then this big gorilla picks Chris up, and shakes him! And another guy pulls a gun! Ahhhh! Riot!

We're against the wall, Chris is up in the air, and this guy's got a gun on me and Mick. I go, "Oh, bless it!"

The little dwarf person is the president of Santo Domingo! For God's sake! And he's…. He's laughing! He goes, "No, no, put them down. It's all right. They're all right. Americanos!"

I go, "No, we're English."

"Oh, even better!" Apparently being English is better than being American over there. And he insists on paying for everything.

So, yeah, we met the president of Santo Domingo, Joaquin Balaguer. And his bodyguards. And looked down the barrel of a goddamn gun.

Well…you start to get worried when you're looking at a bloody big gun looking at you. And you don't know, 'cause these guys could just kill ya. Throw you in the swamp, and the alligators'd just take care of the rest. And there's dead bodies in the street anyway, so you know damn well your life ain't worth a thing.

Donna wasn't in the casino. She was very sensible. She was in her suite with her security guys outside the door, James Andersen and his buddy Bob. Our guys are very professional, and they're licensed to carry as well. Donna wasn't in any of the public spaces, 'cause she'd get mobbed. It was just the crew and a couple of the band guys with us in the casino. She stayed in her suite fighting the cockroaches and the lizards, and the…flying things, about that big. You could hear the sound of wings flapping, and you'd go, "What the fuck's that?" They were so big you could shoot them and eat them.

It was chaos. Anyway, yeah, we got out of there all right. Santo Domingo. Good fun. Only someone like us would go there. Nobody goes there. We went to some of the weirdest places. But, as I said, they paid the money.

Donna Treats Us to a Hawaiian Vacation

We did some shows in Hawaii. I can't remember the name of the gig. It's the big convention center, where Elvis Presley played. Big gig, 15,000-seater or so. We sold it out for 3 nights.

Me and the lighting director Chris Dale flew out ahead of the gig. He was my best buddy on tour. Great guy. We tried to fly ahead a lot because that way you can advance it, get all the rigging points, where the system's gonna go, where you want the stage built, what the local equipment is. See, for this gig we didn't take a sound system, we ran one in that was over there, and that all has to be double-checked. You have to know what's going on.

The prop plane was down in Puerto Rico and that area to go island to island. From L.A. to Hawaii you have to take a jet. For me and Chris I booked our tickets first class.

On the way over we were sitting next to Vincent Price and his wife. He heard our accents and said, "Ahhh! Hellooooo chaps!" He's very English, you know. Lovely man. A magic man.

He said, "Let me buy you some champagne!" Of course you can't buy anything if you're in first class, it's all free anyway. But he's insisting on buying us champagne 'cause we were English, and we were in the entertainment business. "Ah, jolly good, chaps! Lovely! What're you doing? What's going on, who's in charge?"

We go, "We're in the music business."

"Ah, well, that's entertainment, it's all the same." And his wife was rolling her eyes 'cause he's pissed as a pirate. God bless 'im. He's very, very nice.

So we flew in about 8 days ahead of the main party. We had rented limousines: Whatever we needed, the promoter paid for. We get into Hawaii and there's a limo waiting for me and Chris, and we went straight to this...heaven.

We stayed at the Kahala Hilton at Diamond Head. It's not a Hilton anymore but it's still a hotel. In those days it was one of the most exclusive hotels in Hawaii. It's got its own private beach, beach bars, kayaks, surfing.... Whatever you want, it's got it, all self-contained. So we weren't staying at something like the Holiday Inn at Waikiki Beach, with all the *touristas*. We were out on this beautifully landscaped tropical heaven. Even in those days we're talking 400 bucks a night, and everybody had their own room.

Jill used to live in Hawaii, so she *knew* Hawaii. And when I told her The Kahala Hilton, she said, "Oh, no, you *can't*. No, no. Nobody can afford that." It's 5 stars. It literally has its own lagoon with its own dolphins. You can sit and have breakfast and throw bacon at the dolphins!

So Chris and I were there ahead, yo ho ho, sitting in the lagoon, drinking, kayaking up and down, back and forward to the bar. Then the main party came over, which included all the wives, girlfriends, kids, the band, the crew. Donna paid for everybody.

It was brilliant. Fabulous! When the main party came over, the girls'd come out of the rooms, and we'd have the chairs set up and everything. Then we'd kayak along the lagoon to the bar, right? Order a tray of drinks, get back in the kayak, paddle back down the lagoon with this full tray of bevvy, and crash into the shore. We'd stagger ashore without losing anything. There's some photographs somewhere of it all, God knows where. Probably Donna's got them.

Ah, it was an easy gig! It was a good gig. I mean, the rigging, the actual technical side of it was relatively easy. And it was all local people who were putting the equipment in, so all we had to do was shout and scream. We didn't actually have to lift anything. Thank God! Because 12 mai tais for breakfast with a bit of Cornflakes is serious business. We just had a great time.

It was very, very nice. And everything's set up; when you're in a gig for 3 days, you don't have to offload, unload, set it up. You're there. You just go in in the afternoon, do a sound check, check all the gear, all that stuff, and you spend all day on the beach with your girlfriend or your wife. Nice one, Donna! She even signed for everything on the room. God knows what the room bill was. I'd hate to think…! But that was Donna being generous. She was so cool on that stuff. We had been on the road a *long* time, and it was toward the end of a grueling tour. We were going to Japan from there, 'cause it's halfway. So we were shattered. Everybody was just shattered, but, you know…Hawaii! Say no more!

Reunited with My Sisters

While Jill and I were living in West Hollywood, my sisters got back in contact with me. I hadn't seen them in years, not since I'd left Apple. They came down to London once or twice while I was still with Apple. Diane actually did a little bit of work for Apple, some bits and pieces, nothing serious.

Then I just disappeared. Like a gypsy. "See ya. Gone. Bye." Didn't tell anyone, just went. Very inconsiderate.

Diane tells me it was the fall of 1983, or maybe it was 1985. I'd been out of town with Donna Summer, doing some gigs or something. Jill was working downtown in the fashion biz. I'm back in town between gigs just sitting at home, and the phone rings. I think it's the office, or one of me mates, and pick it up.

"Hi there. Is this, um…Bryan Rooney?"

"Uh…yeah."

"It's your *sister*!"

"Good *God*!" It's Diane! "How are you? What? Who? Where?"

So what Diane had done is, she'd actually bought one of Donna's albums, because she was into the disco stuff apparently. Then she was looking at the credits on the album, and it says something like, "And special thanks to Bryan Rooney for taking care of" whatever, the equipment and doing all that stuff. I got credit on the album. And me bloody sister reads this little tiny ant-size print, "Bryan Rooney."

She phones Casablanca, Donna's record company, in L.A. And Casablanca and our management company were in the same building on Sunset Boulevard. So they transfer my sister to the bloody management company, and she says, "Ah...this is Bryan Rooney's sister, and I need...."

And they just give out my phone number! "Oh, yeah, Bryan Rooney. Oh yeah, what a great guy! Here's his number."

Then Diane just phones me...good God! I was happy to hear from her, yeah. But I was a bit confused.

We got it together, and she flew over with my other sister, Sue. We all had a big reunion, and became best friends again.

Managing Donna's Sound Stage in L.A.

Donna had a studio, her own sound stage, down on Vine Street. I was in charge of that side of it when we weren't on the road. I used to rent it out for her for other bands to rehearse in. Elton John used to rehearse there. It was a great sound stage. You could put up a sound system and lights as prep for touring. It was a big place, with offices, and that's where the management company was, Susan Munao Management.

Booby Daniels and I are good friends. I met him over here, in the United States. He was with Elton John, with Bobby Reid. I met him through Bobby, who I knew through Elton John. The Beatles, Apple, Elton John—they're all mixed in together you know. Did the visit and partied together and went to the clubs together. So I knew Bobby Reid from England. He's a really good stage manager, and was head carpenter for Elton John. He was in charge of all of Elton's sets: the hydraulics, the curtains, the backgrounds, all of that stuff. Bobby is really good at that stuff. Really, really good. Very together. Right now Bobby's back on tour now with Nine Inch Nails. Great roadie.

Booby was the drum roadie for Elton's drummer Nigel. He'd done John Bonham's drums too. Even now he's the best drum roadie on the planet. Booby and Bobby were good friends, both Scottish. I met Booby over here in America down at the King's Head pub. He's just a great guy. I took him out with us for a couple of gigs with Donna. He had a spare couple of weeks, and I needed a drum roadie, so he came out with us for a few gigs. It was all the usual stuff, "I know you, you know me, help." We'd all help each other out.

Booby's a great guy—if you can understand a bloody word he says. He's got a really seriously heavy Scottish accent, a brogue. Give 'im a pint of Guinness and you can't understand him. Well, I can understand him, but for anybody else you'd have to put on subtitles on the bottom of the screen. I'm from Liverpool so I understand him. If I revert back to my accent, my original accent, you wouldn't understand me either. I mean, I've modulated my accent some since I've lived here in America, because I couldn't get around. I couldn't even get gas in my car or buy a loaf of bread when I first came here. Even now I have to have my wife Jill order for me in Mexican restaurants because they're only used to the American accents. [With heavy Liverpool accent] "A coupla a en-chi-lah-dahs, lad." They're like, "What?"

Born Again? Nah!

Ahh…what gigs. That Hawaii/Japan one was a *great* tour. We did really well. Brilliant tour. That's the tour we had a 36-piece orchestra. They went on our crew plane too. They thought it was brilliant. They didn't want anything to do with traveling on Donna's flying church. Yeah. During that tour she became a Born Again Christian.

Donna's family, from Boston, were on the road with us. During a gig her father would come up to me and tap me on the shoulder and tell me, "I don't like the sound tonight."

I've got the biggest sound system you've ever seen! I've got two 36-channel boards imported from Germany, right? I've got racks and racks, and more racks and racks, of special effects. My soundboard area would take up half a backyard. Plus the lighting system is next to me. And here I've got this guy from Boston who's a butcher, tapping me on the shoulder, saying, "Sure don't like the way that cymbal sounds."

You know what I was thinking. "Who the fuck are you? Go back stage and have a Boston beer, or something. Just leave me alone."

I had 8 or 9 semi-trucks full of equipment! And there's cousin Billy Bob or whoever it was, wandering around, going "Oh, what's that? Why isn't that pointing this way?" I've got dozens of guys from the local union I'm trying to manage, plus my own crew, etc., and here's a couple of Donna's relatives going, "Oh, look isn't it nice!" "Why is that yellow?" "Can you make that one move?" And, "It's too loud!"

I'm like, "Back off! Get off my stage! I'm the production manager! This is not a holiday camp! Get your ass off my stage. NOW."

It got to a point one particularly lunatic evening where I had to go to Donna and say, "You've gotta tell your family to stay away from me and my crew. They can't just wander around during a show. You've gotta get them outta there. You've gotta keep them away from me, my techs."

Donna knew I was seriously annoyed, so she gathered her family together in the hotel suite one night and told them, "You've got to keep out of Bryan Rooney's way. And you're not allowed *on* stage, you're not allowed access to anything to do with the production. Because Bryan tells me it's going to be dangerous."

And, well, that shit can be dangerous. You've got how many thousand volts running through main cables, and these people are kicking stuff, going, "Oh, isn't this fun! I'm Donna Summer's 2nd cousin on her 3rd auntie's side."

I'm like "Back off!"

And Mick is like, "Who are these people? What do they want?"

I had to put the word out, to put them off. It was very intense. So when we got back to L.A. after the tour there was already a bit of tension.

Donna's parents were Born Again Christians. And they just kept on working on her. She'd had a hard life until she became famous. Donna didn't mind a drink or 2, nothing serious. Sometimes she'd have a drink with the lads. She'd come down the bar and buy everyone a round of drinks, didn't think anything of it.

And then the Born Again Christian stuff took over. It was all about, "The Lord wouldn't like that." And "No swearing."

Well, the only way you can get through a day on the road is by fucking swearing, you know! "What the fuck did you do that…?" "Oh, ya twat!" It's part of the gig, just to release your goddamn energy and frustration, you know? It's a heavy number. Ask anybody on any crew. You've gotta be able to be able to release the pressure, 'cause it's a *lot* of pressure when you're doing that stuff. Then all of a sudden someone's saying, "No cigarettes, no drinking, no drugs."

We get back to L.A. after God knows how many months on that particular tour, 9 months, I think. We're back in Hollywood, I'm back renting out her sound stage for her. When we were off the road I was on retainer, paid by Donna's office. With the crew, when we weren't on the road the crew was the crew and they'd go and do their own thing. You wouldn't—couldn't—pay the whole crew when you weren't on the road. They'd go pick up different tours and things.

I'd just done about 7 years with Donna. I'd done my fair share of getting her famous: I put her shows together. I designed her stages, all the hydraulics, all the levels. I did the quick-change room inside the stage for her costume changes every 3 songs. I designed the stages with all the stairways, all the sound baffles, the hydraulics.

Then a memo went out: "Attention production management staff" —i.e., me. It went something like, "We've found the Lord. We're going to turn the sound stage that we have into a church. No drinking, no smoking, no drugs." Donna, God bless her, has turned Born Again Christian through the influence of her family, her parents.

Nice, isn't it? That's brilliant, that is.

You know, under those conditions I'd just end up a basket case. I would have been in hospital with stress. You've gotta release it, you know? If you're brought up in England, Liverpool, the pubs, and in Germany, in London, and the Merchant Navy…, you can't just stop, and go, "Oh, yes, Praise the Lord."

Now, I was brought up Catholic. But the Catholic church doesn't have a problem with drinking—or they wouldn't have anybody in it. I mean, if you told a Catholic priest he couldn't drink, he'd quit. They drink every day at the altar, right? "Body of Christ, blood of Christ," and the "blood" is consecrated wine. Then after mass they go to pub and talk with the parishioners.

The Born Again Christian crowd are very conservative. It's, "I've found God *again*, and I'm sorry for all the mistakes I made until this point, and I'm going to change. And so is everybody else." They're *way* heavy about it, because they think it's the only way to redemption. You've seen them: "Praise the Lord! Jesus saves!"

Well…fine. God bless 'em. I can't fault anyone for that. But I didn't wanna become a holy roller. I was a Catholic. I was an altar boy. I did my share. I believe in God. But these people, once they get the message, they're all, "Ha ha, we're better than you, we're clean-living…."

Get lost. *Really*. To me, her staff and everyone were all yes-men, yes-people. Born Again Christian is fine, but *don't* force it on somebody else. I'd never force Catholicism on anyone. Why should I? I don't give a monkey's wedding what somebody else thinks. Black, white, green, yellow, Chinese, Arab…do what you wanna do. But don't force it on me, 'cause I ain't gonna take it. Somebody tells me I can't smoke, and I can't have a drink, and I can't swear? My attitude is, "Well…fuck off!"

So, well, it just became…not intolerable, but…the gulf was too big. The tour was over, and renting out the sound stage was quiet. There really wasn't much happening. The best thing was for me to split. See ya!

Roadie Dad and Video Mum

So after working for Donna Summer, for a while I did some gigs locally, meaning around L.A. I did some more work for Ringo again, taking care of him, his cars. Did little bits and pieces with other bands. Nothing serious. I did some work with Bobby Reid, who put me on a tour with a band called DeBarge.

When I came home from the DeBarge tour, da dah, Jill got pregnant. Jill was traveling a lot at that time. She was with a company and was going back and forward to Hong Kong, China, Europe. Even though she was pregnant, she was still zooming up to several weeks before we had Gemma.

We lived in West Hollywood for 10, 12 years or something. It was a little apartment with 1 bedroom, one of those old 1930s Spanish apartment buildings.

I ended up working for a friend of mine who was one of our neighbors and also one of the managers of a company called Lexington Scenery and Props. They built movie sets and things. He convinced me to come and work up there with him in North Hollywood. They've got a big shop with hundreds of people: carpenters, painters, scenic artists. They needed people on the transport side to get it organized, deliver and set up sets, go back and forward to the locations and all that.

And that's how I found Santa Clarita. We were doing a movie over in one of the movie ranches on Placerita Canyon or Sand Canyon. It was a big old cowboy ranch, literally, with a big old Spanish hacienda-type house, and stables and all that. Did a lot of cowboy stuff there. I was delivering and setting up some sets over there and one day I just knew Jill and I had to do something about getting out of West Hollywood before the baby was born. I was coming home down the 14 freeway one afternoon, in one of the trucks, and I thought, "This is a nice little valley." I pulled my truck off and cruised down San Fernando Road and Bouquet and all that, and saw all these little houses—and For Sale signs.

I went home and said, "Jill, I found this really nice little community up by Magic Mountain."

She goes, "Oh, good!" 'Cause Jill used to work at Magic Mountain too when I first met her. She used to do those portraits for the customers, sit there with her easel and do a portrait for 6 bucks a shot. I used to drive up Magic Mountain and meet her. So she knew the area, but when she was working here, this place was just farms—sheep and onions and stuff. There was no housing. But Newhall Land took over, and developed it.

So we came out and looked at houses. One afternoon and we just cruised around 'til we found a real estate agent, and she took us around to 8 or 9 houses. Some of them were nice, some were just…stupid. Then we found the one where we live now. And Jill was like, "Um…."

I said, "That's *great*, Jill. Look, it's…," well, it was bright goddamn pink, 'cause it was owned by Cubans. The inside was bright yellow and orange. It was a bit like gaudy for us, but it had a nice big lot, and it's on a really quiet street. There's no thoroughfare. It was a great house, but it looked awful.

They wanted a good price for it compared to some of the other stuff that we'd seen. I talked Jill into it. And then Jill's parents came up and really helped us out with the deposit. They were still alive at that time, God bless 'em. They were really thrilled that we were actually gonna buy a house, instead of renting a goddamn…slum down in West Hollywood. And we didn't want to bring a baby up in West Hollywood.

We got the house June the 1st, 1988, just before my 39th birthday. I moved in and started repainting it. Jill stayed in Hollywood 'til I got it finished. And then Jill came out, and we let the rent go on the other place, and we moved in.

Just under 3 months later, Gemma was born. It was just one of those days…"Uh, oh. I'm going into labor."

"Oh my *God!*" You know, the usual panic. Ah, Christ. But we had it all organized: the suitcase, all that stuff you do. And we went to Lamaze classes and all that and how to breathe…and scream. So I knew what was happening.

The only real problem was that Jill's doctor was down in Beverly Hills, at Cedars Sinai, which is a 40-minute to an hour's drive from here.

We get in the car, straight down to Beverly Hills, and get the doctor over, the gynecologist dude. And then the bloody pain goes away. The doctor says, "Ah, no, it doesn't look like anything's going to happen."

Ah Christ, I'm gonna have to drive all the way back there, and it'll start again. It's that kind of deal.

He said, "Tell you what. Just go walk around the hospital grounds for an hour." So we start to walk, and then Jill starts labor again, through the walking and just moving around.

Back in, he says, "Okay, so that's fine."

Up to the birthing room…. And then the bloody baby wouldn't come out! C-section. *Oh, God*, here we go, right? Okay, fine. So I'm freaked. You know, c-section, split your stomach open and drag a kid out. What on Earth?

They let me in the room. I couldn't see anything because they put me behind a sheet with a mask, and I had all the robes on so's I could hold Jill's hand.

So yeah, I was there when the baby was born. The spanking, the blood, the afterbirth…I saw the whole bloody lot. But Jill needed me, so I was there. Yeah.

We had a baby! Great! Brilliant!

It's Cedars Sinai, you know, Beverly Hills, excuse me. That'll be 10,000 bucks, thanks a lot. Nice one, eh? But we had insurance and all that, and Jill had a nice suite. They put a trundle bed in for me, so's I could stay there, 'cause c-section takes a while to heal. They don't just kick you out the hospital, apart from the fact they want their money. It's like a hotel, with room service.

And it's right opposite the Hard Rock Café, which is convenient, 'cause just as soon as soon as Jill went to sleep, zzzzzp, I'm down the elevator, across the street, in the Hard Rock, "Cognac! Everybody, Cognac! Give everybody a drink of the usual." It was brilliant. Cigars and the whole thing. Yeah, it was great.

Jill's parents drove up. They were thrilled. They had a granddaughter! They were magic. Jill's mom was in tears. Everything was perfect.

We'd just moved into the house as well, and then there we are with a baby! It was without a doubt the proudest moment in my life, my biggest accomplishment—the second one was meeting and marrying my wife. Because I wouldn't have lasted this far without my wife.

In the meantime, Jill's in the fashion business as a designer. She's very, very good. Her career was doing really well, and the company she was working for at the time are like most of these places, all of their stuff's done over in Hong Kong in China. So Jill had to travel all the time: 6, 7 times a year she'd be over in Hong Kong. Or Korea, Japan, England, or Italy.

So the deal was, Jill would carry on with her work. I said, "Okay, that's cool." I'd had enough of the road, I'd had enough of the goddamn music business. And I was tired. I was crazed. I had a baby. So we made a deal. Jill enjoyed what she was doing, her career was doing well. So she'd carry on, and I'd stay at home.

In those days stay-at-home fathers were quite unusual, really. But I wasn't scared of kids. I could burp the baby with the best of 'em, and make 'em throw up, and knew the diaper scene. I had it all down.

I mean, I was a good dad, 'cause I was an old roadie, you know? I knew how to treat people. I knew how to take care of things. So, I said, "Ahh, no problem!"

Six weeks after Gemma was born, Jill was on a plane to go down to Hong Kong, and I was on my own for 6 weeks with the baby. But I was cool.

We made some videos of Jill reading stories, saying "Goodnight," and "Good morning, Gemma!" Every morning, after I'd been up all bloody night anyway with the kid—you know what it's like, diapers and all that. Every night. Every morning I'd put her in front of the TV and play Mommy. Just hit the button and there's Mommy, "Good morning, Gemma! How are you? This is your Mommy," and Gemma would go "A goo goo gah," 'cause she recognized Mommy. Kids are amazing, they recognize things.

That's how we dealt with it: Roadie Dad and Video Mum. It was quite cool. It worked out good. Gemma's quite sensitive now. She didn't go the wrong way, so we brought her up right. I'm quite proud of it. We did all right.

So there I was, stay-at-home Dad. I've done a few things, but I was so tired of rock 'n' roll. Drinking, drugs, falling over…. I was just tired of it.

You've seen throughout the book how many friends of mine have died. Quite a lot of people I've known well have just died! For different reasons, but it's a complicated and heavy gig at times. People just die, for whatever reason.

But I'd come through, and survived it all. I was a bit beaten up, lost me teeth, and I've got scars all over me and shit, but I got through it. Had some great, great times, as well. And I was quite happy just to be at home, and Jill was happy doing her thing.

I mean, we've had our traumas like everybody. I remember this: I went in the bedroom, and Gemma's gone. No baby! Ahhhh! What! She was in there last night! She climbed out the bloody window. She was only like 18 months, 2 years old. Climbed out the window on some bits and pieces, come down the back alleyway, and onto our street! Had wandered over to the neighbor's house and knocked on their door. The little hooligan! The neighbor's coming out, "Are you missing anything?"

"Me daughter…."

"We've got your daughter."

How the hell? She walked to the neighbor's house. Couldn't even talk. Little hooligan.

We did nursery school. Took her to church. 'Cause she's an only child, we did things with other kids. We didn't want her just to be alone, she needed to socialize. That's the way we saw it. So we put her in preschool: It's a society, you learn things, learn how to get along with other kids. For us, it was important. So we did all the right things, read all the books, fed her, brought her up.

Later on when she's in school, there were bad report cards here and there, and Jill goes ballistic. Jill's obsessed with education—which is all right. It's a good thing to be obsessed about. I'm a lot more…casual. I'm a casual dad.

Of course, Gemma's 18 now. And Jill wants me back out, doing something. I could be a gas station attendant or something. HAHA!

So I basically walked away from the music business when Gemma was born. I've been the stay-at-home-dad for these 18 years now. And I'm so proud of my daughter and my wife. It all comes down to my family.

And since my sisters found me again, *now* I have an extended family. I was just so used to just being *me*. Then I'm married, then I've got a kid, and this whole scene arrived from England. And they've got their families and now I'm part of them—Germans, Scots, Irish.

I hadn't really cared about it. I was so used to being alone, bouncing around, responsible for nobody, or to anybody, except for who I was working for. And I made my own schedule. If I wanted to go out and stay out all night, I did.

Then all of the sudden I'm part of this huge tribe. I've got Jill and Gemma, and I take them to England and Ireland to visit everyone. My own family comes over from England to go with us to Lake Tahoe, to Yosemite.

Sickness and Recovery

Then I got sick. My sisters were over for summer vacation when it started, I think in 1999. We rented a house down on the beach in Ventura. So we all went down: sisters, Jill, and Gemma, me.

Literally the next thing I know, is I woke up…in hospital, with tubes sticking out all over me. I didn't have a clue what had happened to me. And one of my sisters is there on death watch. I'd had the Last Sacraments from the priests, *in nomini domini*, God'll take care of you and all that stuff.

"*What* happened?" Apparently I'd caught a disease, spinal meningitis and hydroencephalitis. It moved up into my brain, and put liquid on my brain, which pressured it. There's no real indication. We didn't know.

After I'd recovered enough to speak to people, they said that apparently, while we were down in Ventura, I just disappeared. And they found me just wandering the streets! In Ventura! "La dee dah dee dah," happy as a clown, didn't know nothing, wandering the streets.

They couldn't make any sense out of me, so Jill threw me in the car and drove me back up here to the hospital. I was still breathing, and she didn't want me in hospital down in Ventura.

So they got me up here, and they'd operated on me. They put a pump inside my head, and I've got a little filter, and plastic tubes through my neck into my stomach. The liquid that builds up, that causes the pressure, drains. Even to this day I've never really figured it out. Nobody really knows *how* I caught it, or how you catch it. Some people say it could be a cat, or a dead bird, or something, that gives you the virus. But we never really had an answer.

Thank God I had some great doctors. One of the best brain surgeons in Western America works down in the Valley at Holy Cross, Dr. Sarona, and they brought him in to sort me out. This guy's like the typical mad German professor. "*Ach! Herr lieber* Bryan!" He used to come and see me, and I didn't even know. And then slowly I came out of it after a couple of months in hospital. I looked like an Auschwitz victim. I couldn't walk. Well, I could stumble. And my arms were just bone. I had no muscle. This was about 8, 9 years ago now.

We carried on, slowly. But I was in agony, because all my muscles, after lying in bed for those months.... The doctors didn't wanna do anything with me while I was in hospital because I was in a such a delicate state. So by the time I finally got out, my muscles had atrophied. I had no strength. I had no muscles. I couldn't lift a cookbook. I had to eat with spoons, out of bowls. I was white as a sheet. I looked like a skeleton. Could see my ribs, could see the bones in my legs. It was horrible.

I've gotta do something. This is crazy. You know? I couldn't eat, and with the medicine they'd given me I'd throw up 5 times a day. I still take that medicine every day, but my body's adjusted to it. Initially, anything I 'et, I'd just throw up. It's like bulimia. And the medicine was awful.

So I went to acupuncture, bein' a clever bugger. Baaaad mistake. You think, "Ah, they can do anything." So I go to this bloody acupuncturist, Mrs. something.... I don't mind shots and all that. I think, "I'll be okay, a needle here, there."

Of all my muscles, they decide that it's my shoulders that won't operate, so I can't do any lifts. So she starts there. She gets these clamps, and they're driven by air, like hydraulics. She puts these clamps on my goddamn shoulders, sssst, and they just *squeeze*. The pressure's incredible. She takes them off, and then she taps these needles in. It's *agony*. And then she puts electric charges through the needles. It's like being in a torture chamber! And I'm *cryin'*! I'm in *so* much pain!

Well, the acupuncture didn't work. Bullshit. So I gave up on that one.

Jill was in a health club, a *great* club. And I thought to meself, well, I keep on hearing about aquatherapy sports medicine—water therapy in the pool. Resistance but no pressure.

So Jill took me over to her health club. Within the organization they have medical people, therapists, and all this. So I went in and saw them and they said, "We can help you. We're gonna put you in a pool, every morning, till we get you back."

So 6:30 every bloody morning I'm in a swimming pool. And it's outdoors, so it's quite cool in the morning. I bought a wetsuit. I just do repetition, exercising, and they have balls and floats and weights. One whole year I spent in a pool, every single day. I was like a raisin. And slowly, ever so slowly, it worked.

Then they took me out of the pool and put me in the gym on real stuff, *gradually*, ever so slowly. They were very careful with me 'cause they knew I was in a bad way. They were great people as well, really kind, really nice people. Not bastards, not nasty or superior. They actually cared about you. I was really pleased with that. And they got me back, got me strength back. It got easier and my body started accepting the drugs better. So that was a bloody miracle, actually. My doctors at the hospital were thrilled. Put on weight again, I could eat with a fork, and kept it down. I could walk again.

And I could drive again. 'Cause they took me bloody license away 'cause apparently I had a stroke while I was in the coma. That's what nearly killed me. They got me through that one, but they have to report that to the DMV. You're listed as disabled. So they took me license away.

But I got it back. I had to go and prove I could drive, so I had to go and take another test. No big deal, just drive around the block. You know what it's like here: Anyone can get a license. The cat could get a license in America. It's stupid. "Turn right, okay, turn left, ahhh, well done, there's your license, off you go," and there you are on the freeway, anything you want. Can't even speak English? They give you a license. It's crazy.

Relapses

And then of course I had relapses. They still don't know why. I've had 3 brain surgeries. About 18 months or so after the original operation, same thing again, and off I went into a coma for 6 weeks. Back to the hospital, more surgery. But I came through that really quickly, I got away with that one. Between the coma and brain surgeries I was in hospital for over a year.

At one point Jill asked me how I wanted to be buried. My sisters flew back "just in case," they said. But I think God said, "I'm not havin' *him*!" Or, "Stay down there for a while, I have to get ready for you."

In hospital I came to out of the coma and this priest was giving me the Last Rights. He give me the wafer, which is the body of Christ. I said, "And what about the *blood* of Christ?" Which is the wine, right?

The pump filter failed. It's a little mechanical valve-type thing, and it just stopped working. So the pressure built up again on my brain instead of draining to my stomach. So they put another one in. And off I went, again. That's cool.

About 2 years after that I got really ill again. Something else happened to me. My stomach expanded; it looked like I was pregnant. When it all came down, Jill was in Florida so I was full-time with Gemma. I just got worse and worse. I went to the local doctor clinic, and they said, "You've gotta get to a hospital."

I said, "Well, I can't. My wife's away and I've got a baby."

They said, "Well, you're gonna die if you don't get yourself into surgery, or something. You've got to go to a hospital."

Fortunately, a good friend of ours had a real nice house down in Glendale way, and she took Gemma. I went back into hospital and collapsed in the waiting room. I couldn't breathe. They cut my throat open, put me on ventilators, and rushed me off into emergency surgery. And I was back in hospital for another couple of months.

The liquid from my brain had been leaking. It's supposed to go into your stomach, and then you pass it when you go to bathroom. But something had gone wrong with the tube, and it infected my stomach.

When they got me out of surgery again, they were putting *huge* syringes in my stomach to draw out the fluids, and it came out like…green bile. Oh, it was horrible. So they had to clear me up for that one.

Then they were putting cameras down my throat. They put you out first even though it's a little camera. They'd send cameras down my throat, and they put cameras up me anus. That wasn't fun. God, I was in bad shape yet again. But they pulled me though. It was close to 150,000 bucks in bills. We have insurance, but we have to pay our percentage.

Now I've also got diabetes and a hernia. I have to have 4 shots a day of insulin. But my doctor's from Liverpool! I couldn't believe my luck. So I made him a shepherd's pie, an English/Liverpool dish. He said, "Ah, brilliant!" And he gave me this new insulin pen. It's like a fountain pen instead of a syringe. I'm so excited about it. It's really cool. You don't have to refrigerate it, just keep it room temperature. You just dial in the amount you need for the shot, and there's a microfine needle you just dispose of. It doesn't even hurt. Brilliant!

I just wish…Jill and Gemma didn't have to go through it…. Gemma thought Dad was dead. As I said, Jill at one point was thinking about making funeral arrangements, 'cause they said "He ain't comin' outta this one." Me sisters and all flew in from England. But I just came through it—blithe spirit, you know. It was a bit heavy, but we did it.

But now everything's grooving along. I'm getting bored. And Jill's right, as I said earlier: I should go find some kind of work now that Gemma's finishing high school. I've gotta go and do something. I don't know what, though. I'll have to find something to do. Jill and Gemma are doing well. The dog's happy, the cat's happy. I've got a couple of decent friends. Can't complain!

I Survived

I survived. The main thing out of all this I've been through is that I survived. I moan and whine, and it *was* hard at times; some of it was grueling. Especially in the early days when I was just a roadie.

I made good money…but I spent a lot. I made great money when I was with Ringo. But with the lifestyle…. They'd buy a round of drinks and it's nothing, it's pennies to them. I buy a round of drinks with that lot and it's all Napoleon Cognac at 80 bucks a shot, and it's your week's wages. But you're part of it. I'm not very good with money. Jill is in charge of the money. And we went on vacations, we did a lot of stuff. We 'et out every other night, at 5-star restaurants, "Yoooo!" Stuff like that. We've got a nice house, couple of cars.

Going from that lifestyle to being a stay-at-home dad was a relief. But now I could go back…if it was the right gig, the right position. Yeah, I'd go back out. But I wouldn't go back out doing anything physical. I'm not capable of it. Mentally, I've got all that knowledge that I could still use. I know how to get things done. If the right thing came up…yeah, I'd go back out again. Maybe. For a couple of months.

'Cause nowadays they don't do what we were doing. The goddamn pop stars nowadays…to them touring it's a hassle. In my days, you did it to sell records and to earn money. The Stones still go out and all that. But you don't see many people going out for 9 months out of the year, you know? It's too much. I'm like an old man, "In *my* day, before the war…" HAHA!

We went out, and we toured. We really toured. We fucking did it, you know? We fought our way up and down the countries, across the countries, laughin', screamin', shoutin', swearin', fighting.... It was a battle. But we enjoyed it! It was like, "*Yeah*! What's next? Back out on the road now?"

I never really worried when I was on the road. I never had conniptions, or nerves. I saw guys on the road crew have nervous breakdowns 'cause of the pressure. I've seen musicians fall over the pressure. I've seen stars collapse.

But me and a lot of my mates, we were all old, hardened Liverpool London bastards. It was just another gig, "Let's do it!" We had responsibility. We were the guys who made it happen. If it wasn't for us, half of these bands wouldn't have sold a single 45, if we hadn't got the bastards out there and put 'em in front of people. We made 'em look good, made 'em sound good. That was our mission. Kept them safe. What they did in their own spare time was their problem.

Out of them all, my favorite artist was Ringo. Still is. I've met loads and loads of people throughout. Some of the biggest people you've heard of, I've met: actors, actresses, Tony Curtis, all that crowd. I've met them, sat down at dinner with them all, drank, talked. 'Cause I was always included: Ringo always included you. He wasn't just, "Sit in the car and wait for me." You were part of the gig, you were included. So I've met a *lot* of people, but Ringo is a lovely man. Taught me a lot as well. He's got a lot of wisdom.

It sounds like I'm sucking up or whatever, but I'm not. 'Cause he knew I was a bastard as well! You know, I didn't mind shouting at him. He'd shout at me, and I'd shout back.

He'd go, "Where've you *been*, you bastard?"

"Oh, mind your own business." Stuff like that. Then we'd just go and do what we had to do. He'd shout at me but it was more like your older brother, though he wasn't that much older than me. But he'd obviously done a lot more than I had. And he's a lot richer for starts, you know! But he treats people well. Yeah, he's still my fav.

As far as being a roadie, when you go on the road it's kind of insular. You're in your own little box. You don't *know*. You ain't got time for TV, news, or the newspapers. You don't know what's happening on a political or planetary scale—the real world, as they say. You lose touch. You're in this globe that just rooooooolls along with you in it, you know? And whatever happens, *bang*! "Oh, okay, another buckle, let's deal with it." That's all you care about. You're late for the aeroplane, or the flights are late, or the busses broke down.

Although the job backstage is important—because without the backstage you can't get the stuff on stage going—in reverse, if there's nobody on stage, there's no backstage! It doesn't matter who you're working for, if they're not in the lights, or they're not creating, doing their songs, selling tickets, and making money, you ain't got a job.

Drugs and alcohol were part of the business then. For all the fun, games, and privileges that you gain from being famous, or being around famous people—the money, the house, the car, the girl—there's a *lot* of pressure, and it's all the time. You're under pressure 'cause you have to perform, you have to deliver. And that pressure can lead to lots of drugs, lots of drinking.

The same applies to the artists' road crews. A lot of my good friends are dead because of the pressure and how they tried to handle it. You know, 18 hours a day on the road—for the artists and the crew—is long and grueling. And studio work is long and grueling too.

To anyone who thinks it's like a walk in the park, "Oh, look at me, the star," throw a few amplifiers around and off we go: It's not like that. It's a heavy gig. It's a serious business because of the money involved. The money and the pressure bring everything else along—the drinking, the drugs, the abuse to yourself. It's not an easy thing.

You have to have a certain attitude to survive. I've seen people go down the tubes because there was just too much going on, too much pressure, constantly. It's not easy. And even if you go out to ease the pressure, like David Bowie bought an island, God bless 'im, there's still pressure. At least he's got his own island. Sensible guy. But if you're in a hotel, or you're just walking on the street, it's just constant "You! You! You!"

The best thing to do is don't join! Don't get in if you can't handle it, because it'll do you over really good. Though really I don't think I have any right to give people advice because it's their life.

I was just lucky. I bounced from one good scene to another. Some of it was hard, but I had great friends, friends that have lasted. Even though many of 'em are in England, we talk constantly. Some of the guys are living here in L.A., quite a few of them. Some of them are even on the road right now with current artists! They're still good friends. Jill and I'll go for a barbeque, play with the dogs…normal stuff. Well, normal-ish.

My mates, Liverpool, Apple, The Beatles, Ringo, Harry Nilsson, Keith Moon…they made me what I am! Did they really? Yes, they did. I wouldn't be where I am today without that crowd, and all that lunacy, anxiety, worry—and the pats on the back, the love, the hugs.

God bless you all! God damn bless ya, forever, and ever, and ever, because of what you did for me. You probably didn't even know you were doing something for me at the time, but in retrospect ya sure did.

It was fabulous. It *is* fabulous. I have a beautiful wife and a great kid—a beautiful daughter who is learning Japanese, of all things. She loves it, and she's good at it. I'm proud of her, and proud of my wife.

Jill and I will be married 30 years coming up soon. There's something special you get your wife for the 30th anniversary, some special kind of gem or something, isn't there? I'll have to find out.

I had a life! I still do. So you'd better sell this bloody book, so I can get back to where I should be! Buy meself a Bentley.

Right.

And look: These are not joints. I have to roll my own cigarettes. They're just regular cigarettes.

That's all I've got! Can I go home now?

Coda

From: Diane Rooney
Sent: Tuesday, December 19, 2006 9:15 AM
To: Vince Falzone
Subject: RE: Christmas Chaos

Hi Vince,

Life is never what you expect it to be—we're just trying to sort out flights to L.A. I don't know if Jill has been in touch or not so you might not know that Bryan died suddenly on Saturday [December 16]. A massive heart attack they think.

Fortunately I was at Sue's over the weekend when she got the telephone call so it was a comfort to be together and try to come to terms with the news. He had so many health problems it's possibly better for him that it all happened very quickly, but a tremendous shock for those left behind. We are waiting to book tickets out to L.A. to be with Jill and Gemma. As yet Jill doesn't know when she will be able to hold the funeral so until that's sorted we can do nothing. I'm back home just now to repack and we're not sure when or where we'll be in the next few days.

Sue and I are so pleased that he's finished the book and we are so thankful that you persuaded him to tell his story and turn the memories into a permanent memoir that others might find something of themselves in.

Take care have a good Christmas and treasure your family because we never know….

Hugs,
Di

Mass booklet front and back covers designed by Gemma Rooney.

Coda

Death is nothing at all. I have only slipped away into the next room. I am I, and you are you. Whatever we were to each other, that we still are. Call me by my old familiar name; speak to me in the easy way which you always used. Put no difference in your tone; wear no forced air of solemnity or sorrow.

Laugh as we always laughed at the little jokes we enjoyed together. Pray, smile, think of me, and pray for me. Let my name be the household word that it always was. Let it be spoken without effect, without the trace of a shadow on it. It is the same as it ever was; here is an unbroken continuity. Why should I be out of mind because I am out of sight? I am waiting for you, for an interval, somewhere very near, just round the corner.

All is well.

♥ ଓଧ୍ୟ ♥ Eulogy for The Life of Bryan ♥ ଓଧ୍ୟ ♥
by Diane Rooney

For those who don't know me, I am Bryan's eldest sister Diane and before I begin I would just like to pass on a couple of thanks. To Jill for all she has done for Bryan, to my sister, Susan for organising the church service, for my brother-in-law David for singing and helping to keep those of us with frogs' voices mostly in tune. To Gemma who has worked tirelessly to produce the order of service you have today. I also thought you would want to know that Bryan, with the help of a recent friend Vince, has only just completed his autobiography—so lots of Bryan-style stories to read when it is published.

Bryan Paul Rooney was a larger-than-life character who has enhanced all our lives with his vivid imagination and outrageous personality. This is just a thumbnail sketch from the perspective of one person, but I hope that you will find some resonance with the man you knew.

He was born on the 3rd of June 1949 to Kathleen and Richard Rooney and was the middle of three children. It might be said that we had difficult lives since Dad died when I was 6, Bryan was 4 and Susan just 1 year old. Mum was left as a widow to bring us up alone and she died when Bryan was barely 17. Despite such tragic circumstances we all had an extremely happy childhood. Without television we read incessantly and invented all manner of adventures for ourselves. Fortunately we lived close to Alder Hey, a famous children's hospital, because Bryan's adventures often ended in a drama of one sort or another. He fell out of trees, off moving buses and in an unsuccessful attempt at levitation, fell between two chairs. All generated open wounds, varying amounts of blood, and required numerous trips to Alder Hey Hospital for surgery and stitches. That he grew up at all was something of a miracle, as exasperated relatives would often comment —"The devil looks after his own!"

An important aspect of his childhood was the time he spent as an altar boy at St. Dominic's Parish church. In those days the mass was always spoken in Latin. Bryan loved the sound of the liturgy; he remembered and repeated sections of this throughout his life. You will find one of his favourite Latin phrases on the front cover of your order of service. (**In Nomine Partris, et Filii, et Spritus Sancti. Amen.**)

He left school at 15 and pleaded to go into the Royal Navy. Fortunately, since Bryan later discovered he was prone to seasickness, Mum refused to sign the 12-year contract and instead used her influence to secure him a place in the Merchant Navy where he served on passenger liners running between Liverpool and New York. I have a vivid memory of him coming home with the most exotic rosy red apples big as grapefruit, the like of which we had never set eyes on before.

In the 1960s – and this might come as a shock to those from the USA, but Liverpool was the centre of the universe. Like all teenagers during those days Bryan had a whale of a time. He may not have been a rebel without a cause, but he was a rebel with intent! Like the Beatles he grew his hair long, which got him into a great deal of trouble with his employers and in Bryan's opinion caused much ado about nothing! He rode his friend's scooter without a license and landed in jail. He cut up his sister's jacket to make a fringed waistcoat. He also cut up my only winter coat to make a bomber jacket. He was a trial and a tribulation to us all, but returning home from one of his trans-Atlantic crossings he presented me with my first expensive grownup perfume—Chanel No. 5—the cost of which was beyond the dreams of avarice and the scent of which reminds me still of his generosity.

At 20 Bryan joined his best friend Kenny Smith in London and toured Europe as a "roadie" for well-known bands such as Procol Harum. When he returned to the UK, Kenny used his influence to land Bryan a job with

Ringo Star and the Beatles. During that wonderful hot UK summer in 1976 I stayed in the Beatles flat which Bryan was renting. Like most men he had done an impressive job of cleaning a small area in the middle of each room. The corners and cupboards contained the unimaginable, but the whole place was filled with flowers and the perfume just about knocked me out.

At the end of that particular summer he disappeared to the USA intent on managing a newly formed British band—Natural Gas. Sue and I lost track of him for several years, but eventually after a series of phone calls in 1985, I managed to track him down. We discovered that he worked for Donna Summer, had married Jill and acquired doting in-laws in the form of Thelma and Jim. The following summer, filled with trepidation and expectation, Sue and I made our first trip to the USA. We arrived at LAX exhausted, over-excited, and then spent a fraught 20 minutes waiting for Bryan to arrive. He turned up in due course and escorted us not to any old car, but a luxury stretch limousine beyond our wildest imaginings. We certainly travelled in style to his West Hollywood home.

Jill turned out to have the patience of a saint and over the many years of marriage this was well and truly tested. As you know Bryan wasn't a saint, but a man with many faults like us all. However, his Irish Liverpudlian background provided him with the ability to charm the birds off the trees, let alone the lesser mortals he encountered in his daily life.

Bryan may have walked with many Rock Stars, but the lasting love and support that he needed during the years of ill health came from you, his friends, and particularly from Jill and Gemma, whom he adored. I recall many years ago, when Gemma was only 6 years old, being dragged into her bedroom to watch her sleeping. Bryan thought she was the most adorable perfect daughter that had ever been born. That he loved Jill was beyond dispute, and their 30th wedding anniversary, which would have taken place this coming February [2007], was a testament to their lives together.

Sadly, in later years Bryan could sometimes be kinder to strangers than to his own family, and like Oblio and Arrow from Harry Nilsson's LP, Bryan felt he had lost the point. But the point is that Bryan enriched our lives with his animated personality—going out with Bryan was a trip into the unknown—even a visit to the local shopping mall could be tinged with magic. He was totally outrageous in his interaction with any and all that he met. Strangers were engaged in conversation and could become friends for life. He gave much of himself; he was a catalyst who could reveal the uniqueness and extract the best from others.

In times of stress I have found this section of a poem by William Wordsworth, **"An Ode to Immortality,"** to be a great help:

Our Birth is but a sleep and a forgetting,
The soul that rises with us our life's star
Hath had elsewhere its setting and cometh from afar.
Not in entire forgetfulness and not in utter nakedness,
But trailing clouds of Glory
Do we come, from God who is our home.

The clouds of glory that belonged to Bryan blazed a trail through our lives and into our hearts. I hope you will treasure his memory always, forgive him his sins, AND never forget the outrageous rogue that lightened our lives with charm laughter love and sometimes the totally unexpected!

16th December 2006

From: Kenny Smith
Sent: Thursday, January 25, 2007 7:45 AM
To: Vince Falzone
Subject: Poem Selection

Dear Vince,

I hope you & yours are well & are enjoying this new year….

Regarding the poem: It was Bryan's sisters who showed it to me. It was written by Canon Henry Scott Holland 1847-1918, who was Canon of St Paul's Cathedral. It seemed perfect for the ceremony. I think it would have been what Bryan would have chosen himself.

Best Wishes,
Kenny

Meditation/Farewell Poem Read at Bryan's Memorial Service by Kenny Smith

Death is nothing at all. I have only slipped away into the next room.
I am I and you are you. Whatever we were to each other, that we still are.
Call me by my old familiar name; speak to me in the easy way which you always used. Put no difference in your tone; wear no forced air of solemnity or sorrow.

Laugh as we always laughed at the little jokes we enjoyed together. Pray, smile, think of me, and pray for me. Let my name be the household word that it always was. Let it be spoken without effect, without the trace of shadow on it. It is the same as it ever was; here is an unbroken continuity. Why should I be out of mind because I am out of sight? I am waiting for you, for an interval, somewhere near, just around the corner.
All is well.

As Bryan wished, his ashes were spread at sea by his family and friends in a small private ceremony.

Bryan was proud that his peers considered him a pirate. They explained to us that the way he went about his job and getting things done was far from the normal route—more like a pirate's. For the sea ceremony, friend and fellow roadie Bobby Reid specifically chartered the Black Pearl and flew a pirate flag. Longtime Liverpool mate Kenny Smith dropped the pirate flag in the water while Bryan's wife Jill and daughter Gemma released his ashes as we all bid farewell to Bryan Rooney.

From: Vince Falzone
Sent: Friday, April 06, 2007 10:50 AM
To: Jill Rooney
Subject: RE: No Subject

Jill,

Trust me, *BackStage with Bryan Rooney* will be part of what I do in this world. I have a commitment with Bryan; this book and project will go as far as I can take it.

During the boat trip, part of his ashes blew up on me, as to say "What's left of my life is entrusted in you now." He said that to all of us that day....

VF

For more information on the BackStage project,
to watch video clips of Bryan Rooney telling his stories in person,
or to order a DVD of Bryan's interviews with Vince Falzone
for this book, visit
http://www.BackStageStory.com.

Printed in Great Britain
by Amazon